Annie Fields

How to Help the Poor

Annie Fields

How to Help the Poor

ISBN/EAN: 9783744797580

Printed in Europe, USA, Canada, Australia, Japan

Cover: Foto ©Lupo / pixelio.de

More available books at **www.hansebooks.com**

HOW TO HELP THE POOR.

BY
(Annie)
(MRS. JAMES T.) FIELDS.

TWENTY-SECOND THOUSAND.

BOSTON:
HOUGHTON, MIFFLIN AND COMPANY,
New York: 11 East Seventeenth Street.
The Riverside Press, Cambridge.
1885

"Though I bestow all my goods to feed the poor, and have not charity, it profiteth me nothing." — *St. Paul.*

"The grand doctrine that every human being should have the means of self-culture, of progress in knowledge and virtue, of health, comfort, and happiness, of exercising the powers and affections of a man,— this is slowly taking its place as the highest social truth." — *William Ellery Channing.*

"No historic event is so important as the advent of a conviction, of a new truth. These convictions of the human soul build up institutions, change the course of events, and alter the tendencies of human affairs; and among all convictions there are none so strong, permanent, and unconquerable as religious convictions." — *James Freeman Clarke.*

NOTE.

THIS little manual does not propose to deal with public questions. It aims to give a few suggestions to visitors among the poor, and to lead all such visitors to attend the conferences which now are held weekly in almost every district of our large cities.

In these meetings, they will reap advantage from the experience and knowledge of others who are endeavoring, like themselves, to lighten the burden of the unfortunate. Especially, we believe that such meetings will awaken a wider interest in the hearts of well-to-do people,— an interest strong enough to increase the number of visitors to the homes of the poor.

Every page of this book is a prayer for more helpers, and aims to show that such labor is neither too difficult for us, nor one from which any household can feel itself altogether exempted.

CONTENTS.

    I. WHY ORGANIZATION BEGAN, ... 5
   II. HOW ORGANIZATION BEGAN, ... 14
  III. WHAT A DISTRICT CONFERENCE IS, AND HOW TO CREATE ONE, ... 26
  IV. WHAT A VISITOR MAY DO FOR CHILDREN AND YOUNG PERSONS, ... 44
   V. SUGGESTIONS IN BEHALF OF THE AGED, . 66
  VI. INVESTIGATION, ... 78
 VII. INTEMPERANCE, ... 92
VIII. VISITORS AND VISITED, ... 107

I.

WHY ORGANIZATION BEGAN.

"Give to him that asketh" is one of the most direct commands in the Christian Scripture; doubtless, in some form, the same command may be found in every scripture since man began his race with man.

The slow growth of moral civilization is only now beginning to unfold the true significance of this law, which is found to stand side by side with other laws belonging to it and explaining it. These bring us to consider the Example from whom we receive our doctrine. We find him living the life of an utterly poor man, who could give neither silver nor gold, yet whose bounty was unceasing. He taught his followers to speak of themselves "as poor, yet making many rich."

"Give to him that asketh," therefore, should be the true motto for this revival in benevolent work which we call organized or associated charity, whereby we learn to take hold of each other's hands, and, forming a breakwater thus against the rising waves of pauperism, find ourselves strengthened into better ways for relieving suffering.

Formerly, when the knight rode out from his castle, he scattered largess as he went, and the people bowed and worshipped the hand that shed down the golden rain; but, when the giver of the gold had passed, they crept into their wretched huts and lived little better than the beasts of the field. As civilization advanced, and castles were destroyed, and men gathered into large cities, trade and commerce increased, and equal chances were given to equal strength. Then the idea of brotherhood among men began to develop. It had been prophesied in the holy places, but at last it was becoming a visible truth in the mind of humanity. Equal worth was seen to be allied to unequal strength, and the growth of love to man produced fellowship and sympathy with suffering. The simplest and least thoughtful, or least spiritual, methods were first seized upon in the earlier times for the alleviation of poverty and its ills. Community of goods, gifts of gold, gifts of land, every temporal method was essayed, and all to no good end. Those who had no gold before, seemed to have still less, and to be worse off than ever, after the gifts were exhausted. The larger the city, the more munificent its expenditure, the darker its poverty and its degradation. Even in these later times, when the idea of civilization has begun to creep "into the study of imagination," a friend has related substantially as follows her experience during one day.

With the early morning mail came a letter from ——— Association, asking for a generous yearly subscription. The names of good men and women were on the list. She read that all cases were carefully visited who applied for aid; therefore, she enclosed her contribution. By and by, we shall see how this money was used.

Another letter was then opened from a woman in Lowell, who had heard this lady's name, and wished "her advice and assistance." The woman had a mortgage on her house, and she sent names of well-known persons in Lowell who would help her with certain sums, if she could make up the full amount elsewhere. The request seemed quite reasonable, because the woman should keep a roof over her head, if possible, having three children. On the whole, my friend decided to make up the deficit of about two hundred dollars. Later on in these pages, I propose to consider another method of disposing of such a case.

A third letter was from a woman who wished to learn to play the harp, and desired to insure her life for that purpose. At this moment, a man called with a paper signed by the mayor and prominent merchants, stating that he fell down a hatchway a year ago, and had required help ever since. Here, also, money was given. I hope in these pages to return also to this case.

Presently, Mrs. X. went out. She was one of the managers of a sewing-circle and a trustee of a Temporary Home, and, before returning in the afternoon, she performed her usual labors in both those positions. Going hurriedly along the street, she was accosted by a child who looked very cold, and who asked her for a cent. It was so little! She gave him a bit of money, and so reached home, her day's work done.

By and by, we will follow this doing out into its detail, giving a simple statement of what was effected by her generous expenditure of time and money. Mrs. X. herself did not feel satisfied. She could not see that anything was accomplished. Apparently, tomorrow must be the same as to-day, bringing much weariness and little fruition. She remembered, too late, that she had intended to buy on this day a certain picture. The artist needed to know that some one cared for his work, and her own children would be better and happier for having the beautiful scene before their eyes.

The thought came back, also, that an evening-school for boys, which she had long hoped for (seeing how much care is needed in city life, for boys), was still far from being established. She saw more and more plainly that she was not yet working altogether in the right direction, since there seemed absolutely no harvest after all her labor.

One day, Mrs. X. discovered from a book which fell into her hands that the subject weighing upon her mind — of how we may best use what we possess, both of time and money, in behalf of the unfortunate — was not a problem belonging to herself alone. It had already become a vital question first in Europe and later in America.

She read of a city in Germany — in which country much good thought is developed —

which had been divided and subdivided into manageable sections and where the poor are all placed under the supervision of companies of visitors, men and women, who go to see the needy and advise with them, in order that educated and sympathetic interest may be brought to bear upon their condition. By this means, it was discovered that the poor and unhappy drop out of sight and lose their way in the world. Therefore, the effect of bringing friends to the friendless has proved almost miraculous, especially during the life of the good man who first tried this experiment at Elberfeld. The result was greatly successful in that place. His work brought the new life which springs from every living seed. Later, Dr. Chalmers achieved a large measure of success in Glasgow, introducing practically the same idea, though possibly it was also original with him. From that moment, the movement was established in the world and can never die out of it. It beseeches humanity to give. Day by day this cry is reiterated, Come and help us! Give us of your time first, then, if you see fit, of your money. Give to him that asketh enough of your attention to find somebody or to pay somebody, if you cannot go yourself, to discover the real condition of the sufferers. There need be no beggars in our American cities. Labor is wanted everywhere, especially educated labor; nowhere is the supply of the latter equal to the demand. But the education of public schools at present does not bring labor of the hands into sufficient prominence; and it is a fact to be considered that governesses and teachers often earn smaller wages than professed cooks and dressmakers when the latter are skilful in their business.

Meanwhile there is a large proportion of the people crying continually, "Give to us." What they really need is a chance to learn how to work, and sufficient protection, in the mean time, from the evils of idleness, drunkenness, and vice.

Miss Octavia Hill writes: "I do believe that our almsgiving has been cruel in its kindness. It is for the sake of the people themselves that I would see it decreased, yes, even put down altogether. I believe they would be richer as well as happier for it. For the sake of the energy of the poor, the loss of which is so fatal to them, for the sake of that intercourse with them — happy, friendly, human intercourse — which dependence renders impossible, seek to your utmost for better ways of 'helping them.'"

This is why organization began with us. A cry was heard from men and women needing a chance in this new land and seeking to be rescued from their misfortunes.

Dr. Joseph Tuckerman was one of the first men in Boston who brought to light the important "difference between pauperism and poverty." His life was passed in endeavoring to awaken our people to their duty, and to the necessity of wise and organized effort against pauperism. In this labor for the poor he says, " We must identify ourselves with the transgressor, through that sympathy with which nothing short of a strong sense of our own sins can inspire us "; and he adds, " A few judicious and energetic minds, combined and resolved to accomplish all they can and may for the suppression of pauperism and crime, could accumulate in this world a better treasure than all their wealth, let them be rich as they may; and in a few years might do more for the advancement of society than without these services would be accomplished in half a century. ... Only by creating a feeling of relationship and connection between different classes of society ... can we ever bring about any great and permanent melioration of the condition of the poor, any great and permanent means for the prevention of pauperism and crime.

"'Faith alone can interpret life; and the heart that
　　aches and bleeds with the stigma
　Of pain alone bears the likeness of Christ, and can
　　comprehend its dark enigma.'"

II.

HOW ORGANIZATION BEGAN.

"How organization began" signifies not only the need from which it sprang, but the form it assumed. The form in Boston is as follows: —

First, the Registration Bureau.
Second, the Board of Directors.
Third, the District Offices.
Fourth, the Agents.
Fifth, and chief in importance, the Volunteer Visitors.

The Registration Bureau is like a room in a large public library, with the private history of individuals, instead of books, carefully arranged on cards which are kept strictly from the public eye; with its library upon the various branches of this wide subject of how best to help the unfortunate, its tables where gentlemen and ladies may consult together, and, more important than all, its Registrar, ready to give intelligent information to those who apply.

The story of the birth and growth of the Registration or Central Office is worthy of record. It is now a basis on which intelligent assistance for the unfortunate can plant itself with hope of success, so soon as society understands its value. When the public begins to serve the poor by first inquiring what is known about them at this office, and when newspapers cease to print appeals for individual needs until the same thing has been done, the true value of the office will be understood; but, while money is wasted on private applicants in whose behalf there is already a large public appropriation, it is not possible to obtain a sufficiently generous sum yearly to foster the best and largest growth of registration.

"The Registration Bureau may be called a clearing-house of information. All reports of relief are kept on cards alphabetically arranged, and there are on file now more than twenty thousand. There is no publicity about this work, and the cards are strictly limited in their use to the detection of imposture or the aid of a family."

Speaking of the important question of church co-operation, Robert Treat Paine, Jr., one of the founders of united service for the poor in America, and under whose fostering care it has grown to its present value in Boston, writes:—

We ask the churches to register all the relief they give; and some of them are ready to do so, and believe it is wise, especially when they find that these facts are kept private. But many of the churches decline, owing to the sacred relation existing between themselves and their own poor. In these cases, we ask them to send their workers to consult the registration in our office; and this they are usually ready to do. The result is a benefit to us as well as to them. It is an advantage for them to know from what other sources their poor are drawing relief, and, conversely, it is our interest to know that that church is also aiding such a family.

Upon this subject, we read in the excellent *Hand-book for Friendly Visitors among the Poor of New York:*—

It should be remembered that all religious bodies recognize their obligations to provide for the poor of their own parishes, and often possess the most intimate and intelligent knowledge of an applicant's circumstances.

Therefore, great care should be taken not to interfere with their treatment of any case belonging to them; and, to avoid the possibility of this, every one who belongs or pretends to belong to any congregation should invariably be referred to it.

All Hebrews should be referred to the Society of the United Hebrew Charities, which society dispenses all synagogical charity. All baptized Roman Catholics

How Organization Began. 17

are members of the parish within whose limits they reside, and should be sent to their priest or to the President of the Conference of St. Vincent de Paul in that parish. All Protestants should come strictly under the same rule, and be dealt with only through consultation with the relief authorities of the parish to which they are fairly affiliated.

The management of the organization in Boston is vested in a board of twenty-two directors, ladies and gentlemen, who meet always once a month, and more frequently in emergencies. In this number are included the Chairman of the Overseers of the Poor, the President of the Boston Provident Association, the President of the Society of St. Vincent de Paul and of the Roxbury Charitable Society. The other members are persons chosen because they are known to have done or tried to do some practical labor for the poor, as well as because of their intelligent interest in the subject.

The district office may be called the home of the agent. Here duplicate registration cards of reference are kept respecting the poor of the district; here information may be found about persons needing employment, especially that of men and children who can work only a part of the time, and therefore cannot be advertised or sent to an intelligence office. These offices are arms, as it were, of the Industrial Aid Society, which may be called a kind of central bureau for employment of this nature. Here the volunteer visitors may find the agent any day, or meet each other at the regular meetings called conferences, which occur weekly.

The agent becomes a connecting link for the volunteer visitors who come daily for advice and assistance. When a family is in distress of any kind, there need be no delay in getting relief, because the agent is always ready to consult with the committee, if necessary, or is able by constant experience to know how and what to do immediately.

The struggle of the volunteer visitors under the various district committees has been a brave one, and the exhortation "to give to him that asketh" is at length bearing fruit; but it is slow fruition, because there must be growth; and, if such work is to be really useful, the service of many persons must be accepted whose work is necessarily intermittent. "This must be done in order that we may secure a sufficient number of workers, and not waste, but gather in and use, all the overflowing sympathy which is such a blessing to giver and receiver. With our volunteers, home-claims must and should come first; and it is precisely those whose claims are deepest and whose family life is the noblest who have the most precious influence in the homes of the poor. But, if the work is to be valuable, we must find some way to bind together those broken scraps of time, and thus give it continuity in spite of changes and breaks."

This we believe we have done in establishing agents in every district who are assisted each by a committee of men and women. Certainly agents and committees are yet very far from understanding the full scope of their work, but knowledge is increasing every day, and the reform is moving on because the foundations are sound.

One great difficulty in advancing any public work of such unobtrusive character is that of finding a sufficient number of unselfish persons who will take hold of it. "I believe that educated people would come forward, if once they saw how they could be really useful and without neglecting nearer claims. Let us reflect that hundreds of workers are wanted; that, if they are to preserve their vigor, they must not be overworked; and that each of us that might help and holds back not only leaves work undone, but injures to a certain extent the work of others. Let each of us not attempt too much, but take some one little bit of work and, doing it simply, thoroughly, and lovingly, wait patiently for the gradual spread of good." In our present method of helping the poor by associated and organized labor, it is found that a little time will go a great way. Two hours a week on an average, the year through, is all the time that need be given by a visitor who is busied with other duties and yet wishes to do something to help the unfortunate. Within this brief space of time, more good can be achieved than is easy to describe; and who cannot save two hours for such a work? I know many persons give more time because it is theirs to bestow, and because their interest grows and thrusts aside other things; but this is no reason why others should withhold the mite they possess.

The lack of organization in behalf of the unfortunate was deeply felt in Boston, and the work has been ardently started. Its present value and its future existence depend entirely upon the way in which the well-to-do people accept their yoke of service.

"The burden is light," but it is indeed a burden, and one not to be undertaken in any frivolous spirit. It is distinctly the work pointed out to us by the Founder of our religion; and, in so far as he is loved and believed in among us, his service will not be forgotten.

One of the important results of this sympathetic inquiry into the true wants of the poor has led to new views respecting what is called "out-door relief,"— that is, the giving of money (or its equivalent) which is raised by taxing the people, if the applicants come under certain rules and laws.

Mr. Seth Low, of Brooklyn, N.Y., has said upon this subject: —

> Is it not worth while, in these days of prosperity, for communities large and small, all over the country, to try the experiment of abolishing public out-door relief? Private benevolence seems preferable to public relief, because it is almost always inspired by a higher motive, and therefore more apt to consider the good of the receiver, because it contains within itself the limits to which it can be carried, and because such relief is less readily sought after by the recipients.
>
> A remarkable illustration of variation in out-door relief in our Western States is seen in Centre Township, Indiana, in which is the city of Indianapolis. In 1875 and 1876, the township trustee distributed nearly $90,000 a year. Since that time, a new trustee has found $8,000 a year to be sufficient. It seems hardly doubtful to a stranger that the private benevolence of

Centre Township could cope successfully with all the real need without the latter small sum.... The subject of out-door relief is too vast in its extent and too intricate in its relations to be treated dogmatically by any one. This present contribution to the theme is submitted in the spirit of one open still to learn from those who differ as from those who may agree with its conclusions.

These are, briefly: —

That out-door relief, in the United States, as elsewhere, tends inevitably and surely to increase pauperism;

That in towns and cities it is not needed;

That even in villages it can probably be dispensed with.

In thinly settled sections, its evils are at the lowest ebb, while its benefits at the same time are greatest. If coupled with the condition of work in return for relief, which in the country ought to be easy of accomplishment, out-door relief in the country would probably be free from serious objection. On the same basis, it is relieved from its chief harmfulness everywhere.... In some States or sections of States, the office of overseer of the poor is at the bottom of the political ladder. The overseers are chosen for short terms, and are expected to serve party or personal ends. It is needless to say that, in the hands of such officers, out-door relief is an instrument full of danger to the common weal. Long terms of office may help to modify the evil, but there is no effectual remedy while the administration of the poor funds is controlled in the interest of politics. Where this is known to be the case in any city or town or hamlet, for the sake of the poor, for the sake of the locality, for the sake of the country, let civil service reform begin there.

The foregoing consideration of the form of organized work for the poor brings us back to Mrs. X. and to the conditions which made it a necessity.

A poor woman came to her door one day asking help. Remembering her many dissatisfactions and disappointments in trying to benefit others, Mrs. X. simply took the woman's address and told her kindly that she would inquire further into her condition. She went as soon as possible to the office of one of our oldest and largest societies, only to find the name as a recipient among eight hundred others who had been referred to one visitor. This "case" was credited with quarter of a ton of coal and shoes for a woman and two children, without further comment.

Mrs. X. discovered that volunteer visiting had gone out of fashion, and that the expert, with his four or eight hundred families to visit during the year, could not be expected to grapple with any details. The "system," good enough in itself, had drifted utterly away from its early purpose, and had almost lost sight of Dr. Chalmers' wonderful work, which had been the inspiration of its founders.

Mrs. X. then went to another society. This one was less catholic in its grasp, and concerned only respectable widows. She found her applicant was known here also, and received her rent regularly from this benevolent fountain-head. She went into the rooms of a sewing-circle adjoining, and found her friend already there, returning last week's sewing and receiving more. On her way home, Mrs. X. met a friend, and was relating her morning's occupation, when the lady replied that she had known this woman, who was a widow, for many years. She was surprised to know of her call at Mrs. X.'s door, because she had made the woman understand that she herself always stood ready to give her what she required. She was an excellent person, and she would ask her about it.

On parting from her friend, Mrs. X. determined to visit the woman. Turning into a court, she rapped at a side door of a comfortable tenement. It was twelve o'clock. A man with shirt-sleeves rolled up, just in from his morning's work, was sitting down before a dirty table, on which was a huge slice of fried beefsteak and some potatoes. Two uncombed children were playing about the floor, and a general air of dirt and disorder prevailed. Excellent health pervaded the place. The woman was somewhat abashed and discomfited by this speedy return of her visit; but, after a brief explanation from Mrs. X. that she wished to understand her needs more clearly, she came away. Something, surely, needed to be done; but what was the something? One visitor with hundreds of cases could not prevail against the evil. Mrs. X. believed that volunteer visiting might at least begin a reform. The attempt was made, and has proved successful so far as it has gone.

This is "how organization began,"—not hurriedly and as a new thing, but as an intelligent outgrowth from old methods which were leading to no good end.

III.

WHAT A DISTRICT CONFERENCE IS, AND HOW TO CREATE ONE.

In the government of a State, we consider the question, Who shall be its officers? to be one of primal importance. So, in the administration of charities in a city district, no rules can be laid down which should for a moment challenge our consideration, compared in significance with the necessity of obtaining the right persons to fill the committees. In the past, the question has been, "Will he do it?" in the future, the query will be, "Can he do it?" Improvement in methods has, in part, wrought this change; but advance in morality, more than all, demands that the best force the community can afford shall devote at least a portion of its energy to grappling with the problems presented by the unfortunate of great cities. This unfulfilled labor is the religion of the present and the future. It is the first duty of the Central Board of any organization, and one never to be set aside for matters of secondary importance, that persons of ability be sedulously informed of the need of assistance, and constantly beckoned to the front. Not as figure-heads, nor to lend their names, but to give such time as they can spare to strict performance of weekly duties; this being far more important to our advance than any gift of money. Without underrating what money can do, we have learned from the past, as well as the present, that, if the gifts of sympathy and energy are withheld from the work of the Associated Charities, wealth may be pronounced useless to perform the service.

The conference of a district is composed of three parts: *First*, the District Committee, to which special reference has been made in considering the need of active intelligence in this service; *Second*, the Representatives of various societies and public or private Officers working among the poor of the vicinity; and, *Third*, the Visitors. This body constitutes a conference. One of the valuable effects of such a body has proved to be that the distinctive gifts of both men and women are required to accomplish the ends proposed. The comparative ease with which we grasp difficulties in Boston, from this perfectly natural union, is to be remarked. We have no separated committees. We have silently recognized the fact that in this business, because we are dealing with social questions and those of the family, we have need of each other.

We believe in the value of a weekly meeting for each conference,— the committee to come together one hour before the moment of the meeting, in order to look over the business to be presented, and to dispose of such cases as need not be brought before the larger company. The agent will have time to ask questions and give advice, and the committee can thus bring itself into order and harmony, which will serve to expedite the business of the following hour. I will not give here the order of work already laid down for guiding the administration of a conference. So far as this business can be reduced to form and put on paper, it has been done, and may be found among the publications of the Associated Charities in Boston; and we feel assured that every district conference will find it greatly to its advantage to follow the printed plan as closely as possible.

The relation between the agent and visitors is one that has been often discussed; but

District Conferences.

we must beware of rules and of red tape. We have to deal with different agents and a large variety of visitors. Some excellent agents are far less able to satisfy the needs of the visitors than others. In such cases there may be special service of another kind which is remarkably performed, making it wise to supply this gap between visitors and agent in some other way. Again, the agent may be an excellent visitor, but slow to make efficient record of work really well accomplished. It would then devolve upon the committee to see that this want was remedied. A person of intelligence and unselfishness, devoted to the work, is what is required in an agent. When these qualities are given to the service, incapacity respecting details, in whatever direction, should be voluntarily supplied, if possible, by the committee.

The work of the committee of each district conference includes one branch of labor too often omitted or forgotten. Each member should be informed respecting the public departments of protection for the unprotected: what may be lawfully asked and received in cases of need; what shelter, what relief, what advice, or what methods of transportation; also, what loans may be obtained; where and how children may be cared for, and the best methods for saving.

In short, the committee should hold its seat, not from any supposed superior wisdom, but from a power of which it is perfectly possible for persons of average intelligence to possess themselves; I mean *resource*, the ability which knowledge can give, prompted by sympathy, to turn quickly when called upon for relief, and to answer, " If the conference considers this application a suitable one, at this or that place relief may be obtained."

Closely related to this question of organized administration of charity in cities is public out-door relief, or the distribution of money raised by taxation for the city poor, to which, under certain restrictions, they have a right by law. This "right" is one of the greatest of man's inhumanities to man. How is the law to estimate, for instance, a woman's capacity to take care of herself, or the injury to her children from receiving a pauper's fund? Questions of relief which visitors find most delicate and difficult to decide are complicated by the demand upon public moneys made by a large proportion of the poor.*

In this country, where every kind of labor

---

* See quotation from Mr. Low in previous chapter.

is needed, and more of it, at lower rates, is constantly in requisition, it is the blind leading the blind and all falling into the ditch together for us to allow public money to be bestowed in what are called settlements by law, instead of being given after investigation, and according to the individual need. What the people require is education, beginning with the lowest forms, in order that money invested in their behalf shall be anything but a future disgrace to our nation. By the lowest forms of education, I mean industrial education in its simplest development,— the use of the hands and feet for some common good.

It should be carefully observed by the officers of a district committee that their position, as such, has nothing to do with the management of loan systems, or savings, or tenements, or any form of relief. Their business is to understand where such systems exist, to discover if well administered, and to keep the roadways open between them and the needy. Of course, their influence will be invaluable for holding all such institutions up to the best working-point; but, by virtue of their office, they are examiners and indicators, and must carefully avoid the dangerous mistake of losing sight of their first duty in **any** such detail. Each member will have as much to do as one person can well perform, under ordinary circumstances, to obtain the proper information and communicate it, especially when we remember that no officer is considered entirely exempt from the practical experience of visiting the poor.

The simple idea of a conference is that various individuals come together for the purpose of getting each other's advice and knowledge. Thought and care are required to make such meetings interesting and profitable, and how best to do this is a question to be kept continually before the committee. The meeting should not only be agreeable to the visitor who has a chance to talk, but the case in hand should be made interesting, if possible, to the whole company, which is apt to include some persons wholly ignorant of the people talked about. I know it is difficult; but I am convinced, if we keep this end in view, we can advance much in this respect. There should be no talking back and forth among the visitors, but the chairman and agent should hold the business in their hands sufficiently to bring out the interesting points in turn from those present, giving every one a five minutes' chance during the afternoon for

District Conferences. 33

the benefit of the whole, and thus limiting and passing over suggestions which belong to a more private consideration of any case.

Our watchword is Co-operation. Its practical efficacy can only be fully understood at the conference. A lady visitor hears the secretary read the name of Mrs. Kelly, giving street and number. She responds: "I found Mrs. Kelly well ten days ago when I called to see her last, but the baby was ailing and needing food from the Diet Kitchen, which I obtained for her. I have not been able to visit her since, and I came to the meeting in the hope that you could tell me how she is getting on. The other children were all at school the day I called, and I could not see them."

There is a moment's silence. Then the truant-officer says: "A week ago, I found the Kelly children weren't at school, and so I looked them up; found chicken-pox had broken out among them. She was pretty down-hearted, being a lone woman, and no money in the house, because the sick baby had kept her from going to work. Said I'd call the next day, but was detained; and, when I went the day after, I couldn't find them. The neighbors' doors were locked (they were all at work), and I couldn't understand it—" Just then, a gentleman, who had dropped into the meeting half hoping that he might hear something of this case, spoke up, and described how "One night last week, it must have been Thursday, I was hurrying home from business rather late, when I heard children crying. That's a sound I can't bear long. So I pushed open the broken door of the house where the sounds came from, and went in. Going up the third flight of stairs, at last I found the room, and knocked. Nobody answered; but the children still were crying, so I went in. There lay a woman on the floor in a heavy drunken sleep, just where she had fallen after emptying a mug which stood on the table. Five hungry, sick, miserable children were wailing, and trying to rouse her in vain. It was a pitiful sight, and what to do I did not know. Out I ran, downstairs again, and asked the first police-officer I met where I could find the Society for Prevention of Cruelty to Children. He said he didn't know. I told him he ought to; but, if he would take some money and carry the children some bread and milk for their supper, I would come back and get them, while he could take away the mother. I found it a long distance to the office of the Society, and by that time the hour was approaching for the last train to take me home that night; but the agent was kind and prompt, and sent off at once to get the children. Unfortunately, I have not been in town since, and could not hear anything more of them; so I thought I would drop in here." Whereupon, a quiet little lady in the corner said: "I happened to come into the office just as you left it, and the agent asked me to go with him, there seemed so much to do. When we reached Mrs. Kelly's, I decided to take the baby myself. We carried the two younger children to Auntie Gwynne, while the agent took charge of the two elder. The officer, meanwhile, was obliged to carry the poor mother to Deer Island."

Our agent then told us how her work for the week had carried her to Deer Island, where, to her great surprise and sorrow, she found Mary Kelly, whom she had formerly known as a good, respectable woman. "The poor thing was terribly abashed and grieved at her situation, and explained how a neighbor, seeing her discouragement, had thought to comfort her by bringing her beer. Little by little, yet faster than she was aware, the habit of taking beer had grown until she was mastered by it. The kind of beer, too, seemed to have dangerous elements in it such as make this drink harmful; and before she knew it her senses were stolen away, and she found herself at Deer Island. So I said, seeing how wretched she was, that I would try to get her transferred on probation to the Massachusetts Home for Intemperate Women in town, where her friend and visitor could see her. After we had assured ourselves of her desire to behave well, we got permission from the officers of public institutions to bring her back to town; and she is doing well, and giving every promise of being able to have her home and children some day. I wish the visitor would now take up the case again, and, as soon as the woman ought to be trusted, help her to get work and to establish herself once more. After such a severe lesson, and with a kind friend to watch over her, I think this will never happen again; and she is longing and weeping for her children." The visitor promises to go and see her, and this case ends for the afternoon.

From this illustration, it is easy to see how a party of people interested in the same work can help each other. It is not often that all the intricacies of a case can be followed out in this way at one session, but it is striking to see how many can be settled in one season. In a multitude of counsellors there is knowledge as well as safety.

Many of the Boston districts contain five or six hundred families who receive aid. Of this large number, not more than one hundred and fifty, on an average, are properly visited and cared for by agent and visitors. New cases sent in as having applied for help in the street, or otherwise, and requiring immediate investigation, in order to relieve the mind of the person applied to, who has generously refrained from giving because of our continual appeals to that end,—even such cases have, in a few instances, been suffered to lie over. Is it not easy to see that public dissatisfaction will be the result of such inadequacy, and also that the fault lies, not in the plan, but in a misunderstanding of methods? How can this evil be rectified? It cannot, of course, be accomplished by a stroke of the pen, or in a moment's time. But when and how shall a beginning be made? We ask the agent. The answer comes promptly, "I have as much as I can do to keep the run of one hundred and fifty cases, assist the visitors, and keep up the books." There seems small chance of help in that direction.

How then? *First*, Every new case sent from outside, because of especial application and present need, should be considered by the committee as a duty to be at once performed, either by one of their own body, the agent, or the visitors; one of the old cases being dropped for that week, or fortnight, if necessary. *Second*, For such emergencies, a committee might be formed to be styled "assistant visitors,"— persons who are willing to be called upon to assist the agent in visits of investigation, in addition to the three or four families regularly under their care. A very small company of such helpers will be of great assistance to the committee; but, the larger the number, the less chance there will be, of course, for anything to be neglected. A large organization pledges itself to respond to these appeals from a busy public. It exists for this purpose, and the execution of the labor rests with the district committees. The old excuse of "too many cases in hand" must be set aside. We are bound to understand the general condition of the district in which we work, and to remember that one applicant has as much right to our attention as another, until all their needs are perfectly understood and classified. Of course, better work will be accomplished when we can confine ourselves to one hundred and fifty cases, but that should be in the future. Our first work is to understand the field as it lies before us, to canvass each case, to beseech the churches who are giving alms here and there to send a visitor to the conference and learn what is there known of the family they are aiding. Private missionaries, any one, in short, giving either money or what is called "charity-work" to any family within the jurisdiction, should be, in a measure, one of the district conference, and persuaded to look more closely, perhaps, into the condition of their charge, or to modify their plan of procedure materially in connection with especial persons.

Another measure for obtaining knowledge of families in the district, who cannot be regularly visited for lack of helpers, will be to gather the children into little schools,— sewing-schools, Sunday-schools, vacation-schools, kitchen garden, kindergarten, cooking-schools, or wherever the committee may see opportunity to place them,— and the elders into industrial schools, laundries, sewing, carpentry, and the like. Last year, a weekly evening-school for boys brought in a number whose homes were quite unknown to us; also, at Christmas and other festivals, we may be brought into relation to new families; and, if we confine our attention entirely to our own district, the time will not be long when we shall have the whole number of recorded recipients of relief in hand, and soon very much reduced. But, if a beginning is never made, and our energies are spent in trying to elevate and educate the few, helping them up very successfully, as we may, we shall find a large body straying about the same as ever, begging and imposing upon the community, until we shall become only "the one more society" so much dreaded everywhere, and the end of organization will remain unfulfilled. We must be content for a time to do more than we can,— that is, we must do less well than we can for the few, until we understand the general need somewhat better, and have more help to grapple with it. The rock ahead has always been that men and women in this business lose sight of the idea, and are ensnared in ruts and in details. Let the committee, at least, hold its head above water.

In this connection, the experience of Miss Mary Carpenter, in the ragged schools of England, is worthy our consideration. She says it was with the utmost difficulty she could keep attention fixed upon the lowest strata. The moment her children had opportunity, they were lifted out of their old degradation and became a different class. Teachers and friends naturally wished to keep on with the hopeful cases; but she was obliged continually, as it were, to plunge her own hands down to the very bottom, and bring up those who had sunken there. This also should be the work of our district committees.

The foregoing difficulties and how to meet them turn upon a subject almost too familiar to be mentioned,— the need of more visitors.

"I feel most deeply," writes a friend, "that the disciplining of our immense poor population must be effected by individual influence; and that this power can change it from a mob of paupers and semi-paupers into a body of self-dependent workers." Believing this, any labor among the poor becomes not only a hope which is constantly nourished by success, but it also assumes the form of public responsibility, where every man and woman may do his or her part. Visiting the poor does not mean entering the room of a person hitherto unknown, to make a call. It means that we are invited to visit a miserable abode for the purpose first of discovering the cause of that misery. A physician is sometimes obliged to see a case many times before the nature of the disease is made clear to his mind; but, once discovered, he can prescribe the remedy. How many visitors fail in this long undertaking! We are at a great disadvantage: we go without authority, and often without knowledge; we are met sometimes with distrust and possible dislike. I can only say, in face of all failures, the success has been triumphant. But, looking at the failures, I am more and more persuaded that we are working at too great a loss. I mean our visitors too frequently become discouraged, and, in army words, "we lose too many men." A partial cure for this is to be found in the tenement house system as introduced by Miss Octavia Hill, and pursued in New York and Boston. A proposition for governmental supervision, quoted in one of the reports of the Board of Health, has been suggested as possible and necessary. Such oversight would assist benevolent work in the homes of the poor, immeasurably.

The value of organized charity lies with the visitors, not in the organization; and as in the St. Vincent de Paul Society, from which

District Conferences. 43

we have derived so many suggestions, no officers are exempted from this duty, so with our district committees,— we allow no one to be ignorant of it. Constant experience keeps a continual sympathy alive between the committee and visitors. They all labor together; therefore, their chief desire is to increase their numbers, seeking to relieve each other of too great a burden, instead of the old habit of asking more work from the same visitors. In twenty years after the establishment of the St. Vincent de Paul Society, Ozanam, its founder, said with his dying breath, "Instead of eight visitors, we have grown to two thousand in Paris alone, and we visit there five thousand families." Is our labor to be carried any less far? I believe not. Our methods have improved, our knowledge upon this subject has greatened. It remains for our faith in God and in humanity to carry us forward into victory.

IV.

WHAT A VISITOR MAY DO FOR CHILDREN AND YOUNG PERSONS.

"How to care for the children of the very poor, and often depraved, part of the population of cities," writes Mrs. Lowell, "is one of the most serious of public questions; and, in discussing it, it is necessary to consider the effect to be produced, not only upon the child, but upon its parents and upon the public at large.... The effect upon the tax-payer and upon the hard-working poor man, struggling to bring up his children to be honest, industrious, and healthy, must not be ignored. The tax-payer must not be required to give what he needs for his own family to support the family of his dissolute neighbor, unless that family threatens to be a public injury; nor should the honest laborer see the children of the drunkard enjoying advantages which his own may not hope for.... There should be a constant pressure brought to bear on parents to contribute toward the support of their children; and, as soon as they are able, they should be required to take them back [if they have been placed in institutions], or, if unable or unfit to do this after a given number of years, they should forfeit all claim to them. No child should be held as a public charge for an indefinite time and the parent have a right to reclaim it at any moment. A parent who will not perform the duties of a parent should not have the rights of a parent."

Dr. Tuckerman says: "I am quite satisfied that far the greatest part of the abject poverty and of the recklessness in crime which people either our prisons or almshouses, or which is seen in our streets, may be followed back to causes which showed themselves within the first fifteen or twenty years of life, — to causes which at that period are within our power."

WITHIN OUR POWER. Will the visitors among the poor — the men and women who are hoping "to do something"— bring these words home!

There is now a statute in Massachusetts which reads as follows : —

[*Acts of* 1882, *Chap.* 270.]

SECTION 4. Whoever unreasonably neglects to provide for the support of his minor child shall be punished by fine not exceeding twenty dollars, or by imprisonment in the house of correction not exceeding six months.

It is clear, therefore, that the visitor has the law upon his side in many cases of neglect. What is chiefly required further is to see that laws of this nature be enforced. The moral sentiment of our people has framed the statutes bravely. It only remains for those who wish to succor the unfortunate to see that the abused child obtains the benefit granted him by law.

One of the forms in which the wrongs of children appear is in the neglect of the babies of wet nurses. One who has made a specialty of the care of mothers and infants writes : —

The exceptional care and watchfulness required to save the life of a young infant separated from its mother, and placed at board during the summer months, can only be estimated by those who have undertaken such a responsibility. It would, no doubt, be better for both infant and mother that they should remain together through the summer. And this can often be arranged by having the mother and child admitted to the Massachusetts Infant Asylum or Medford Infant Asylum; but the poor young girl, tempted by the high wages of a wet nurse, and ignorant of the danger incurred by the separation, seldom hesitates in her choice. We are then compelled either to leave the poor baby

What to do for Children.

to its fate,— which would be speedy and almost certain death,— or to expend upon it an amount of time, toil, and care which would suffice to save the lives of ten infants at another season, with the result (which we have now learned to expect almost as a matter of course) that the mother, removed from our influence, separated almost wholly from her child, and taught indifference to her duties and responsibilities by her employer, comes to us at the end of the summer with an urgent request that we will assist her to relieve herself altogether of the charge of her infant, by placing it in some institution,— although a wet nurse is better able to support her child than any of our patients not similarly placed. Wet nurses, therefore, cause us more trouble than any of our other patients, and are the most disappointing of our cases. But this need not be so if the bearings of the situation were understood by the employer, who would then co-operate with us in what is for the real interest of the mother and of her child.

In such service, the idea of the visitor's true work is made evident. She (for this would be a case for a woman) is the assisting and instructing medium between the young nurse and her employer on one hand, and the child's questionable fate on the other.

Cobden said, "There are many well-meaning people in the world who are not so useful as they might be, from not knowing how to go to work." In studying this subject of neglected children, methods of work have been tried which bring us nearer regeneration than any attempts to influence the dangerous classes in any other direction. Here we know "how to go to work."

"I would say," writes Dr. Tuckerman, "to all who wish to do good, whether they have much or little to give to those who are in want, strive to save at least one truant, vagrant, or vicious child, who, if no friendly hand be stretched out, will fall into the abyss either of pauperism or crime."

The taking of children from miserable homes in tenement houses during the summer and sending them away for a week or two "gives a look almost of health" to some who were pinched and wretched to look upon. Air does much, and milk and oat-meal, instead of tea and bad bread, do the rest.

"That these children are alive at all, that fatherhood and motherhood are allowed to be the right of drunkards and criminals of every grade, is a problem whose present solution passes any human power, but which all lovers of their kind must sooner or later face. . . . Hopeless as the outlook often seems, salvation for the future of the masses lies in these children. Not in a teaching which gives them merely the power to grasp at the mass of sensational reading, ... but in a practical training which shall give the boys trades ... and the girls suitable occupations."

Our prosperity seems to be still too great to allow young women to feel any necessity to go into domestic service; or the reason may be a moral one, and lie deeper. The labors performed in bag-factories and other factories and shops are certainly quite as heavy and less refining than those of household service. "To be a shop-girl seems the highest ambition"; but the steps downward from this ambition are frightfully easy. It is, however, a good beginning toward the cure of the evil to have it widely recognized, and to find a growing respect for household knowledge, especially for the fine art of cooking.

House-keepers' classes are forming gradually, where young girls from ten to fifteen are taught everything except cooking, that requiring a separate foundation. To get girls into such schools, if only for a few weeks, often develops tastes and capacities which they could not previously know they possessed, and by which their whole lives are lifted from the old degradations.

For unmanageable girls and those who must be sent to institutions, we have learned after sad experience that a great deal remains to be done. In Massachusetts, the Dorchester Industrial School for Girls took the lead in inaugurating a system of *individual guardianship*. This plan has resulted in a company of State Auxiliary Visitors, who aim to hold personal guardianship over every girl graduating from the public reform schools and institutions. "One whole year before the Auxiliary Visitors began their work for the wards of the State, the Hampden County Children's Aid Association, proposed and created by Mrs. Clara T. Leonard, had taken every child from the almshouse, and provided for all children who might come upon the county in future, by securing committees in every town who should seek out homes and watch over the children when placed. This society has the right of legal guardianship over its wards, granted by the legislature. A certain amount is paid by the almshouse toward the board of those children thus placed out who are too young to earn their own board and clothes."

The report of Mrs. Nassau Senior, of England, a few years ago, describing the lack of power in girls trained in institutions to stand up and take their places in the world, first drew attention seriously to this great topic.

What to do for Children.   51

Above all, such girls need friends; and, without them, they are seen to sink down into the great "criminal sea," which has been largely made up of graduates from public institutions. The stories told by our New England visitors are touching and interesting beyond words. Compared with this work, how petty other occupations seem!

We will turn now to the consideration of another class of neglected youth, and recall the apparently harmless gift of a few cents given to a boy by Mrs. X. Such gifts to street children are sometimes a fountain of life-long evil. If, however, instead of this baleful response, we listen to the real wants of the little child, and gather him up into the arms of love, we have already learned that much will be accomplished. For those who have not yet learned "how to do it," the following truth, pronounced by high authority, will at least show where we must abstain from doing. "Every child," says Dr. Tuckerman, "who is a beggar, almost without exception, will become a vagrant, and probably a thief."

"In Hamburg, at one time," writes Mr. Kellogg, "a police regulation went so far as to forbid almsgiving in the street." Such measures in America would be neither profitable nor desirable; but what is seen to be a necessity is that public opinion shall recognize the wrong-doing in such careless response to those who appeal to us in their misery. Our hope is in and for the children; yet many a mother with four or five little ones, from whom she must be away all day, will lock them up together in a room, under the care of the eldest, until her return. One of the duties of a friend should be to prevent this locking up of children; because there are both nurseries and kindergartens where the little ones can be sent, besides the common schools for those over five years of age. For the mother, eager to get to her own work, the difficulty of preparing little children for school so early is certainly serious. But if she be friendly to the idea, and will take the baby to the nursery as she goes, some kind neighbor will often help the others on their way. Teachers of kindergartens will sometimes call for a child who has no other chance of getting to school.

Although no one case is just like another, human nature being infinite in its variety, it will still be useful to study ways of relief employed by others, and to see what has been

What to do for Children. 53

accomplished. In the hope of gaining usefulness in this way, the following history is related.

There was a family, living in a certain district, where there were two little girls, seven and nine years old. They were under the care of their aunt, who had married their grandfather, and she held papers for the guardianship of the children. She was a French Canadian, speaking little or no English, but expressing great anxiety for the good of her wards to every one who came near her. She was a Protestant, and an excellent beggar in her church and out of it. Everybody loved to be kind and generous to her, both for her own sake and the children's; but one day the grandmother fell ill, and then the friendly visitor who was appointed by a conference of the Associated Charities was able to understand the case more perfectly.

The family was found to consist of the grandmother and her husband, also her father, a son eighteen years old, and the two girls now nine and eleven. They were in debt; but, in spite of this fact, they had a family of pets: there were many poodle-dogs, big and little, a parrot, a cat, and canary-birds; and one day a woman, coming in to warm herself by their fireside, left her baby, never calling for it again; so the baby was included in the family. Four boarders were found to be also of the company; and these eleven human beings, with their pets, inhabited four rooms. The two girls cooked all the meals for the family of eleven persons. They were seldom allowed to go to school; and it was the grandmother's excuses in this particular which first aroused suspicion with regard to the case. When they did go, they had a habit of rushing down two flights of stairs, past the door of a crazy, drunken woman, whom they dreaded, and out into the street, trembling. On their return, piles of the day's dishes awaited their washing. The household duties often kept them at work until eleven at night, and before six the next morning they must be up to get breakfast. They were on speaking acquaintance with all the men in the market-stalls. The boarders would get into fights with one another, and the girls were taught that they must not call in the police, and were even shown how to keep the officers away. The grandmother also instructed them to lie to the boarders and others, when any advantage could be gained; and their clothes were utterly neglected.

"Imagine," writes one who knew the circumstances well, "these girls, with refined and affectionate natures which made them favorites everywhere, leading such a life, and ruled by a woman whose bursts of temper, profanity, and coarseness made her a terror to those who did not know her cowardly spirit. The family had better means of support than many others, and resources which, if developed, might have made them respectably independent. But, in spite of three years of the combined influence of church and charity visitors, instead of the grandparents working harder, they overworked the children in the household service, taught them to beg and deceive, surrounded them with improper associates, and deprived them of their schooling. The result was the girls were growing up to lead unhealthful, dependent, deceitful, ignorant, and possibly still more degraded lives. Various ways were then tried to obtain a peaceful separation of the children from their grandmother, but without success. Hearing the report of the visitor, the conference asked that all 'relief' might be withdrawn from the family. This resulted in the grandmother's allowing one of the girls to be put into a school supported by her church in a distant town;

but in a short time she went secretly and enticed the child away. By this time, the constant labor of several visitors had given us the necessary evidence, and truant officers, relief-givers, and visitors all agreed that the time had come when it was necessary to take these children from their home by force. Assisted by the Massachusetts Society for the Prevention of Cruelty to Children, this was done, and the girls were placed in a public institution.

"We had now checked the 'old charity' which gives outward relief, but develops no inward resources; and we had removed the children from the fearful influences which such charity often fosters.

"The 'new charity' had taken these children away from the only home that belonged to them, and had incurred the responsibility, therefore, of providing a better one. We had placed the girls in the institution, because it is one of the places which serve as hospitals for the moral diseases of children. As soon as the Superintendent thought it wise, the elder girl was placed in a country family, which served as a convalescent home; but the child's moral sickness showed itself by unmistakable symptoms, so that her return to the 'Home' soon became necessary. There she remained some time longer, until it seemed well to try again, especially as an excellent place opened for her,— a home which we knew would give her the combined love and wisdom so essential to the development of a child. After five weeks, the lady wrote that she had seen nothing like deceit in her, and thought her far above the average girl. An opportunity soon offered to send the sister to the family of a near neighbor, and the result proved satisfactory. It is quite possible further changes may become necessary with one or the other, but the way seems fair now to launch the girls upon a respectable and independent life.

"Let us return for a moment to the grandmother, thus suddenly bereft of her children. A chance was found for her at once to support herself by fine laundry work, but this she did not accept. It was then decided to leave her in the care of her church people, who now report her as supporting herself and living independent of relief."

"It were useless," continues the faithful friend who has recorded this history, "to recount all these details, unless we can arrive at some principles of action and plans for the future provision of children thus rudely torn from their natural protectors.

"These principles may be ranged under five heads:—

"1st. The only just reason for taking children from their natural homes is to lift them out of MORAL POVERTY. MATERIAL POVERTY alone is not sufficient cause.

"2d. When there is sign of moral disease, children may be placed in some of the numerous institutions or homes provided for them, which serve as hospitals for the treatment of such diseases.

"3d. Children should not be allowed to stay too long in these institutions or homes, because they will become entirely dependent upon others, and unable to act for themselves. One year may be fixed as the longest term. They should then be placed out in families for convalescence.

"4th. If the moral disease makes its appearance again, the children should be returned to the home for further hospital treatment.

"5th. In selecting a home in a private family, great care should be taken to find one where the children will be taken in a measure for their own sake, not as servants merely. If possible, brothers and sisters should be placed so near that their attachment for each other will be cherished."

We have the record of many families where the children have been taken away from drunken and unfit parents; but, unfortunately, the story does not often extend beyond the Marcella Street Home or some such hospital. Surely, it is strange that visitors should be content to stop at this critical part of their work, when one year flies so swiftly away and a second in any institution will possibly rob a child of the power to stand alone.

The following brief history will be an excellent guide and encouragement to many a visitor who is looking upon the career of some young girl with dismay, if not with despair.

A young American girl, Mary, just twelve years old, excited the strong interest of one of my friends. Her parents were intemperate, and were living at the North End of Boston. She was handsome, fond of excitement and of having her own way, like many bright girls, and she had no restraining influences at home,—if the place of her abode deserved that name.

After visiting the family nearly two years,

all the time having in mind a desire to get Mary to go to service in some kind family, my friend persuaded the father and mother to allow the girl to go where she would earn her board. She had been getting into wild habits and with bad companions. The summer was approaching for the second time when a reluctant consent was won from them; but, after a few weeks of absence, Mary became unhappy, and during the summer vacation of her visitor she returned to Boston. The second autumn found Mary in a worse condition than ever before. She had passed the summer in such amusements as the North End afforded to a reckless little girl. She had sufficient pride to be wretched in the despicable home afforded her by drunken parents, yet her friend did not wish, till other means failed, to deprive them forcibly of their guardianship. The teachers at her school, and others, agreed in calling her the worst girl of her age they knew, and pronounced their opinion that she could not be got out of Boston except under arrest. Her friends felt it would be useless to put her at service anywhere where she was not compelled to stay, and her character prevented her admission to the Dorchester School.

An application was then made to the Children's Aid Society, which places children in families where they will be taught and strictly watched over. This society agreed to take charge of the child, and promised to have a home ready for her if the father and mother would sign a paper giving that society the guardianship for the next four years, and if the girl would consent to go.

Here, then, was a case for influence, and my friend wrote to Mary's father to come to see her. This he did not do, but sent a friend in his stead, to say that he would not give up his daughter. The deputy proved a true friend of the family, and, being a man of good sense, listened to the visitor. He was easily persuaded by her that the proposed plan was the best chance for the girl, therefore he undertook to make the father change his mind. He succeeded in so far as to get his consent to see my friend, and the interview resulted in the signing of the paper by his wife and himself, giving up the guardianship of their daughter till she should reach the age of sixteen.

The next point was to get Mary's consent, as the parents refused to compel her; finally, the friend of the family and the visitor together persuaded her, also, although she knew she was going to a lonely farm-house where she must work and could never come to Boston. Her evil companions did all in their power to keep her; but she went, because, when it was fairly put before her, she did wish in her heart to be good.

The visitor took her to her new home in the uninviting November season. She has behaved on the whole extremely well, and the effect on her parents has been excellent. They were sobered by Mary's loss, and for the sake of her younger sister are striving for a better life at home.

Parents who cannot govern themselves are naturally unfitted for the guidance of their offspring. Girls are to be found everywhere who are utterly untaught in any business of life. They have been compelled to go to school, but they are ignorant of any useful service. They pick rags and sew in tailors' shops, or, if they are especially fortunate, get into a store; but these places are overcrowded, and they can earn a mere pittance by such pursuits. Wherever a visitor can rescue a girl from such a life and cause her to be trained to some useful calling, a valuable work has been accomplished. There are many training-schools in and near Boston, besides the best of training which a well-disposed girl can always receive in the family of a good, motherly woman.

We have been informed by the statistics of the Labor Bureau that there are twenty thousand homeless young women in Boston whose wages average only $4.00 per week. The visitor should learn this statement by heart, and try to save as many girls as possible from this hard fate. "A little self-control would raise the poor into the ranks of those who are really wanted and who have made their way from the brink of pauperism to a secure place, and one where they are under better influences. Above all is this true of the children. A little self-control would enable the daughters of most of these people to rise into the class of domestic servants; and their sons, instead of remaining street-sellers, would soon learn a trade or go to sea, if they cared to do regular work."

There are many societies, plans, and laws for the protection and education of children; but the difficulty of supplanting or supplementing the work of a parent is great, and should be so. Where parents can by any means be brought to support and guide their own offspring, it should be our idea to assist them to do this, since it is nature's law. No help given is so sure of success as the personal oversight of friendly visitors who feel a certain power behind their friendship. The Society for the Prevention of Cruelty to Children, our excellent truant-officers, the newsboys' evening-school, the Law and Order League, all these are ready to strengthen their hands. One of the most hopeful methods of dealing with street-boys is, however, to send them away on farms. From the streets of New York over sixty thousand boys have been sent into the West, who are doing well. What benevolent plan can give a better showing than this?

Let no visitor despair of doing something to improve the condition of neglected children, especially one who lives where there is a Society for the Prevention of Cruelty to Children. Such a society is, however, a helper, and not a place where the burden may be dropped by the visitors. If the officers find a friend who is willing to go with them to the judge and bear witness to the miseries of which they complain, they will find not only co-workers, but a genuine power to assist and relieve. If, however, the visitor drops the case into their hands, and it becomes one of thousands, it must not only wait its turn for examination, but, for lack of proper testimony, it may never come to justice at all.

The hearing in neglect cases is not public, and no lady need hesitate to appear. It is given in a private room; and, as hearsay evidence is never received,—if the visitors really wish to help the children, it will largely depend upon themselves to get what is required. All complaints are confidential.

Where the parents of children have proved themselves unfit for their charge, the visitor may, through the Probate Court, obtain *guardianship* and *custody* of such children. This gives power to find a good home, and to advise for their future.

"Can I do anything more in this case?" a visitor will ask who has taken a woman with three children to visit, and who has been fortunate enough to find work for the mother. Yes, we answer. Do not feel this case is finished until each of those children is in a fair way to make industrious and useful members of society. The inherited paupers of Europe must die and be crushed out on our soil; their children should become our useful and busy compatriots.

V.

SUGGESTIONS IN BEHALF OF THE AGED.

PEGGY O'HARA is now fifty-eight years of age, but she is feebler than her years would seem to justify. With her, as with so many others, poverty, combined with ignorance, and their attendant ills, have induced premature old age. Peggy's husband went to the war in 1860, and soon returned ill. Her father lived with them from the time he was sixty until he became eighty years of age, contributing very little to their support during this period. Peggy could do only the coarsest sewing; and it was through her bad sewing of the soldiers' shirts, by which she was trying to maintain herself and her father while her husband was away, that I made her acquaintance. In the beginning, it was necessary to compel her to take out and do over a large part of her work; to-day, she sews very neatly, but always slowly. She could find very little else to do, however, during the long period when she was confined at home chiefly, with the care of both husband and father, and it was impossible for her to meet the family expenses without help. One friend paid her rent, the overseers found the family entitled to a "settlement," and therefore gave them certain punctual relief, and many givers of occasional doles appeared who managed to keep them comfortable. At length, the father and husband died, also many of the old friends; but begging had been found very lucrative and quite agreeable. Peggy wished to continue her old plan of life, with the hope of reaping a good harvest for herself; but the friend on whom she chiefly depended, having the needs of many dependent persons upon her hands, and seeing at last by her experience that there was a better way, resolved that Peggy must now try to maintain herself. She stated this necessity frankly to her, and said, as she was now left to herself, she must manage to earn what was necessary for her own support. She did not require so much room, and could take some one to lodge with her. Peggy stoutly opposed the suggestion; but, coming shortly after to her friend, in a depressed frame of mind,— having been sent for, indeed, because she was found begging in spite of remonstrance,— she said that she could not live peaceably with anybody she could think of; other women would wrong her and make her life miserable. Her friend listened (understanding Peggy well enough to know this was quite true), then answered, "Well, Peggy, why shouldn't you take a little child to look after, some one of the many motherless little ones we are constantly hearing of?" Peggy thought not, and her friend was for the moment a little discouraged with regard to finding the right thing for her. But, about six weeks later, going to her rooms one day to see how she was getting on without any relief except what the overseers granted in view of her settlement, she found Peggy unusually comfortable and bright, and a little baby asleep in a cradle in the corner. No words could express Peggy's satisfaction. At last, she had found something to love and care for, and her whole appearance was changed. The money she received for its care was just about enough to pay the room rent and for the baby's food, and this made her comfortable with the bit of washing and coarse sewing she found weekly. But, apart from this, even if no money had come from it, the influence of the child itself proved beneficent in bringing cheerfulness into a poor, arid life, which had lost courage and hope and desire, and was sinking under the early approach of age.

Peter Church, as he is sometimes called, is an old Italian of the better class of poor. We found him living utterly alone, in great filth and destitution. He said ten cents a day was all his food cost, because he lived chiefly on macaroni which he cooked himself. He would go to gentlemen whom he knew a little, on the streets or at their offices, and ask a small sum for his support. He had once taught his native tongue in a rudimentary way, but his sight had failed; and he liked to roam the streets at his own will until he was tired, and then at night he would sometimes make a little fire and play the flute. When he first came to our notice, he was becoming feeble. It was getting unsafe for him to go about alone, lest he should be thrown down. He was losing strength from cold and lack of nourishment. Nevertheless, we discovered that he had once tried the shelter of an institution for a few weeks, and had been so unhappy at the loss of his freedom and the constant sight of misery that he ran away on the earliest opportunity. It was a puzzle what to do. For a few months, some friend to whom he had applied for help gave the money to an interested visitor, to be paid out in the very small portions he required. Meanwhile, many plans were suggested for his shelter and protection; but to all of them the independent old man turned a deaf ear. At length, in a kindly talk, it was discovered that the sufferer had relatives in another city. An account of his condition was written to them, and very soon a reply came, saying, though they were still struggling themselves, they would each subscribe seventy-five cents per week, the total proving sufficient for the old man's modest board and maintenance.

The friendly visitor takes sincere pleasure in seeing this money paid out to a needy family willing to take care of him for the remuneration received.

It is a cause for wonder to see how many aged and infirm persons are left to pine away in the attics of cities, forgotten by their own people, and receiving fifty cents a week to pay their rent from some relief society. It is not astonishing that good honest Betty Higdons do not wish to go to the almshouse; but there are many cases where intemperance and uncleanliness have set in, induced by their feeble and solitary condition; and where, when kindly persuasions are brought to bear, they will go to Austen Farm or some other retreat, and once having made the change are grateful and pleased.

I found two sisters living in a scant, squalid fashion. They were Scotch by birth, and had been dressmakers, but had outlived their custom and their usefulness. They were getting small doles which they chiefly spent in drink "to keep up their spirits." They would not tolerate the idea of being sent away, at first. The visitor was firm about it, all relief was cut off, and they cannot now express the gratitude they feel for the care and shelter they receive at a public refuge, near Boston, for aged women.

"Among those who have fallen from fortune into utter penury, and suffered in silence," writes a friend, "are the Grays, two old brothers, Englishmen,— one a good classical scholar, and the other of such ability that he formerly earned several thousand dollars a year in business. He was ruined by a partner. I found him, one day, warming himself by the fire of a sickly little old woman who befriended him and cooked his rye or corn meal once a day. He has eaten meat rarely for years. I had heard of his distress, and forced myself, against his will, into his chamber. I never have seen such utter destitution: no fire, no stove, no lamp, no comforter, no blanket, no pillow, almost no furniture. Many remnants of a sheet had been sewed again and again together, till it was now perhaps three feet wide. What was once an excelsior mattress was now about as hard as a board. 'You do not know what I have suffered here,' said he: 'I was ashamed to let you see it.' To supply all these needs was a pleasure. His gratitude was even surpassed by his unwillingness to be helped. I sent five dollars by a lady for him to make some drawings, but he had parted with all his apparatus, and *refused the money*. He was not a case for the Overseers of the Poor or any public relief. Our conference voted that he should have a pension of two dollars a week, which was enough for his food, as he has his rent free.

"The two dollars were nominally given him for errands for the conference, which he performed most zealously. 'I see through it all,' said he: 'you want me to think I am earning it. Let me do all you can.'

"His literary brother had been poorer still, and, having no fire, frequented a public library where he could read and keep warm; and then, for lack of food and fire, chewed ginger to keep alive. He, too, received a pension, kindly raised by the clerks of an institution which knew him.

"They were about the last survivors of a family which had included a barrister, a clergyman of the English Church, and a merchant.

"Charity sometimes appears hard when it cuts off relief from those able to earn a good support, yet who prefer to beg; but surely it delights to discover and tenderly relieve those who have done their best, and who are left in old age to suffer, unfriended and alone."

A visitor of thought and experience, to whom the foregoing pages had been referred, writes in reply: "The foregoing cases were not all ideally treated. Some of them had been injured by doles, and others by the notion that relief from the city is a right. But such experiences lead to certain *principles* which should be followed in the care of aged people. The first impulse, when we find a white-haired woman living alone, and apparently friendless, is to find some home in whose sheltering care she can be placed. But a home which is not full is hard to find; and the more homes are built, the larger grows the crowd of applicants. Once in, the old person often finds the rules necessary to so large a company irksome, and wishes herself back in her own lonely room. But, the bridge being burned behind her, she remains only half happy and half grateful for the bounty she has received. Means must therefore be sought to reduce the number of applicants, and to confine their privileges to those who really need the kind of care an institution gives. Also, greater consideration is required in order to care properly for those who remain outside."

Mrs. Lowell writes succinctly on this subject:—

We are constantly coming on *chronic cases*, so to speak,— old, or permanently sick, people who can never hope to earn a living. The only thing to be done for such (unless we simply pass them by, as perhaps in the early stages of our work we must) is to provide for them permanent relief of one kind or another,— either put them into a suitable institution, or secure from individuals such regular relief as will place them above the need of casual help, and then see to it that they do not beg.

The following suggestions for the better care of the aged are contributed by a thoughtful friend and fellow-worker:—

1st. By patient study of each individual, and by ingenious experiment of one plan after another, some fit occupation can often be found which shall bring both happiness and profit. Peggy O'Hara's story illustrates this.

2d. If unable to earn enough for full support, the relatives should be sought out, and persuaded to bear the burden, as in Peter Church's case.

3d. If both work and relatives fail, who shall care for this worn-out soul? — we as individuals and friends (to make the end of life peaceful and content for one who has done well his part in the world's work), or we as a body polity, giving the bare necessaries of life to one whose destitute condition is a symptom of disease? To answer this question wisely, a knowledge of the past life is necessary. If opportunities of saving have been thoughtlessly passed by, if intemperance or vice has been allowed control, neither pleasant manners nor the most pathetic pleading should prevent our seeing that to help such a person encourages improvidence, intemperance, and vice in others. If relatives who ought to aid will not do so, they should be made to feel that, because of their negligence, the disgrace of becoming a pauper falls upon their kin.

Aid must therefore come from us as a body polity to protect the community from people infected with moral disease. Such cases should be aided only in the almshouse. Private charity does not do its full part while any other than almshouse cases are allowed to fall into the care of the city authorities.

If, on the other hand, savings have been swept away by misfortune, or slowly eaten up by long sickness; if, in short, no serious fault is behind the poverty that has fallen like a blight upon old age,— we ought to be proud and glad to share our abundance with these stricken ones; and those who have been employers or known the aged people well in any relation of life ought to have the first claim to this privilege of doing good. If to a stranger first comes the knowledge of the need, be it his grateful duty to seek out the old friends. If none can be found, private benevolence must see that the sum necessary for comfort is regularly given. Let not a week of plenty be followed by weeks of semi-starvation, because we will not take the trouble to make our relief regular and adequate.

What can be done to prevent old people from becoming dependent upon strangers? We can encourage thrift, and foster family affection and the sense of responsibility in children for their parents, in brothers for their sisters; and, at least with every applicant for our charity, and often in counsel with those we know in other relations, we can use our forethought to make sure that as many as possible are put in the way of providing not only money, but friends, for their own old age.

How many women left stranded at forty, who have bravely made their way alone, might have been saved the unhappiness and need into which they fall in extreme age, if into the empty heart some other lonely ones had been taken, and a new home, where all worked together, could have been made!

VI.

INVESTIGATION.

THE science of investigation is only half understood by those who believe in it, and only half believed in by the world in general.

"I like his looks" must always be a strong argument, because character carves and sculptures itself on the human face in unmistakable lines; but, in order to learn whether the original value of a face has been raised or degraded by the will behind it, which we call character, is a knowledge no one can get with surety at first sight or without study.

The cry, "What in the world can we do for these people?" comes often to the ear, if not to our own lips. Perhaps we find a family far too respectable for the almshouse, but who seem to be of no use, and, as it were, born without the power to stand alone. What can be done, indeed?

It is a brave heart, and one of much resource, which does not sometimes fail before the need of these helpless creatures. We wonder why they were born, and why they are here in the tumult of city life to be run over by the tide of busy feet. It seems to be the theory of some saintly souls that many people are created incapable, simply as a cross and ladder for martyrs into heaven; and, doubtless, a few may remain for the edification and purification of their stronger-shouldered brethren; but experience shows this percentage to be a very small one,— so small that, as our opportunities for observation widen, we come to believe that every human being can do something, if he have a chance, and is intended to fill some gap in the universal plan.

In order to find this gap and to understand what a man can do who has fallen by the way and failed to find his proper place, we must first acquire some knowledge of his personal and inherited character.

Such knowledge can only be obtained by careful searching and inquiry by a skilful person. Volunteer committees may occasionally be able to do this; but we have only to see how difficult ladies usually find the business of obtaining proper knowledge of the servants they engage, to understand how unfit volunteers often are for this business. Miss Octavia Hill says: "We cannot work wisely without full knowledge of the circumstances of those to be dealt with,— hence, the necessity of investigation. . . . A great deal of the preliminary work is quickly and well done by an experienced person, which it would be difficult for a volunteer to do; neither is it a sort of work which it is worth while for a volunteer to undertake. I refer to verifying statements as to residence, earnings, employment, visiting references and employers. The finishing touches of investigation, the little personal facts, the desires and hopes, and, to a certain extent, the capacities of the applicant, no doubt a volunteer visitor could learn more thoroughly; but that can always be done separately from the preliminary and more formal inquiry."

The following little story will illustrate better the uses of investigation than can be done by any mere description of methods:—

In describing the benefactions and perplexities of Mrs. X., the reader will remember that a paper was brought to her door by a man who had fallen down a hatchway some time before, and had been assisted by the mayor and other prominent citizens, who had given him a paper to show, with their names appended, and the amount of their subscriptions set down.

Mrs. X. carried the name and address of this man to the agent of a district near his abode, and asked to have the case examined. It was found that the accident had occurred ten years previous to his application to her, and that he had become perfectly able to work; but the subscription method of existence had proved so satisfactory that it was continued in preference to returning to hard work.

None of the gentlemen who signed the paper in behalf of the supposed disabled man had ever looked into the case. When, at last, the visitor of the Associated Charities took the trouble to do so, the man was found totally unworthy. He had certainly injured himself at one time, but nobody had looked up the date, and the mayor who headed the paper had been out of office twelve years.

Another history of a different character may also be of use in illustrating the necessity for close observation and scrutiny in order really to help the unfortunate to any permanent good.

One of the appeals to Mrs. X., you remember, was from a woman in Lowell who wished to have the interest paid on a mortgage. It was discovered, after a while, by a friend to whom she applied and who took the trouble to look into the subject, that the house was worth something above the mortgage, and it would be wiser to sell. One thousand dollars was the result of the sale, which money was invested in a small, comfortable dwelling sufficient for the woman and her children and one boarder. They had no debts, the boarder helped to pay running expenses, and the two eldest children began to earn something. By this timely care given to their business, the woman was not only rescued from the position of a beggar, and several hundred dollars thus saved every year, which she had begged for ten years regularly to pay the mortgage, but she was delivered from anxiety, and her children felt an honest pride in keeping an independent roof over their heads.

In one of the first papers published in America upon a better way of helping the poor, wherein the methods so generally adopted since are admirably described by Mrs. Ames, she says: "Wherein does our method differ from others whose machinery is much after the same pattern? Chiefly in the spirit of its administration. . . . It not only requires that every case shall be carefully investigated,— it makes that investigation the main feature in the proceedings; it creates for the community something equivalent to a court or tribunal, which puts each case on trial, looks up the evidence, and seeks to guide its decision by some intelligent principle of reason which has the moral force of law. It assumes that a request for help is not in itself a ground for bestowing it, any more than a complaint lodged in a Court of Common Pleas is ground for giving a verdict to the plaintiff. ... It is made certain that the amount of helpless dependence can constantly be lessened by the careful painstaking and judicial administration of local charity."

The result of failure to investigate is seen every day. The impossibility of finding good positions for persons who are not known, and the mistakes in placing those who are only half understood, sometimes makes us feel that knowledge of character underlies all success, and failure to obtain such knowledge is the best reason for want of success.

In order to give some idea of the far-reaching nature of true investigation, the following history will be of interest:—

One day, a lad about fifteen years old called

at a gentleman's office down town, asking for help to start in the business of selling newspapers. He was originally from England, but was just then recovering from a hurt in the heel received while running an elevator in Chicago. The gentleman, who was a believer in the endeavors and a visitor of the Associated Charities, asked one of the agents to investigate and report to him, when he would gladly give some assistance if it were thought wise. Letters were sent accordingly to England through the Charity Organization Society, as well as to Chicago and Philadelphia, the addresses in the latter cities being furnished by the lad himself. Meantime, another kind of employment was offered him, which he accepted; but he failed to appear at the appointed time. Also, the address in Philadelphia was a false one; but the record from Chicago was good, although it covered only the one month preceding his accident. From the London Charity Organization Society, we learned that the lad's story was altogether untrue. He has a mania for running away and leading a vagrant life. In vain have his parents advertised for him. They are far from being dead, as he says, on the contrary, they wish to send money for his return to them.

They are respectable working-people, and full of grief because of their prodigal son.

While we were waiting for these letters, the lad disappeared. He was heard of once, with his leg bound up, begging at a lady's door, who gave him money. The police were notified as soon as we received the information; and it is to be hoped that the knowledge of his case will spread abroad widely enough to cause him to be brought into a better way of life.

The plan of action agreed upon by the conference, into whose care the case fell, was as follows: The police were requested to arrest the boy as a vagrant, and hold him while the information should be sent to the office of that conference. An effort will then be made to have him placed, by the judge of the court, "on probation," until fitting employment may be found for him, either on a training ship, or by sending him to sea. His vagrant propensities seem to preclude the possibility of any success either in sending him home, which has already been tried, or finding employment for him on land. This case is at present unfinished, certainly; but the first step has been taken, by means of information obtained from his parents through the Charity Organization

Society of London, for rescuing the lad from a life of continued deceit and crime. "The crime of begging," as Edward Denison says, "does not consist in the mere solicitation of alms. The gist of the offence is the intention of preying upon society; and of this intent the asking alms is only evidence,— not proof."

In a valuable paper lately printed by Mrs. Lowell on the subject of "Duties of Friendly Visitors," she remarks: —

> One very important point for a visitor to aim at is to find out all about the man of the family, where there is one. Charities and charitable people are too prone to deal exclusively with the woman, accepting her statement that the man is looking for work. Now, perhaps he is, and perhaps he is not; but the facts should be fully established,— 1st, that he has no work; 2d, that he would be glad to get it. The man and the woman should be seen and advised with together in regard to their present condition and future plans. Where there is a real desire to help themselves, the man will be ready to accept his proper place as head of the family, responsible for its support; and, where he keeps out of the way and lets his wife do the running and the begging, the visitor may well suspect that all is not as it should be.

This is excellent, but now and then we find the trouble lies in the other direction.

Within the past six months, two cases have come before one committee where the incompetence and inertness of the women have chiefly caused the degradation and shipwreck of their large families.

The first is the case of a woman, her brother, and five children, who never asked any help, but who were found by a friendly visitor one day this spring while searching for another family. This company of seven persons had been almost entirely supported for many months by the labor of the two eldest children, fourteen and sixteen years old. Their clothes were worn out. The tenement where they lived was dark and dirty, and despair seemed to be settling down upon the place. It was discovered that the father had gone to the far West two or three years ago, and made a home there. He earned the first year about two hundred dollars, which he sent to his wife, asking her to come to him and bring the children. Her mother was then living, who did not wish to go; therefore they spent the money, and lingered until in a few months the old woman died. He could not send any more money on account of plans he had made to prepare a comfortable home for their reception. A letter was sent westward immediately to corroborate the story. It was not only found to be true, but kind neighbors offered to send fifty dollars in order to bring out the two eldest children. Although this was clearly impossible, these children being the chief bread-winners for the family, an offer was made to raise the rest of the sum here, if the whole party could be received with reasonable hope of employment. After a brief delay, a good woman came from the West with the fifty dollars in her hand; the remainder was raised in Boston; and the party soon left with lunch-baskets and decent clothes, full of hope for this new life in the West. But the mother has been difficult to manage; and, except for the enthusiasm of the children, would have preferred to waste and languish in the poverty and filth of her miserable abode. Except for her fear and incompetence, the whole family might have gone with the two hundred dollars sent so long ago, and her poor children would have been spared much suffering and degradation.

Very like this is the history of another family with a mother who was suddenly left a widow with nine children. They were becoming utterly dependent in the city; but a place was found for them in a factory town, where they had a clean, airy tenement (a beautiful contrast to their wretched abode in Boston), and, what was, for them, a large income. But the mother's total incapacity either to cook a dinner or to buy it properly, or, what was far more important, to train her children, led them into debt. Suddenly, we heard, to our despair, that they had returned to Boston. Their going had given cause to hope for a good future for the children, and their benevolent friends rejoiced in giving them everything for their comfort which could be thought of. Therefore, to find them once more crowded into a wretched hole at the North End and asking alms was indeed a disappointment.

A council was held upon the case; and it was decided that the only hope was in a factory town, and that we must send them off again elsewhere. But how to do it? They could not absolutely be compelled: therefore, what measures could be adopted? We found there were two reasons for their wishing to remain in the city: first, the eldest girl, who was getting beyond all restraint, wished to be in town; second, the mother thought she could get relief from public and private sources. These, then, were the two points of attack; and it was thought well to try both at once. A wise, sweet woman, who has a gift for influencing young girls, was persuaded to try the first. At the same moment, all the relief societies were asked to withhold assistance, in spite of the fact that the family really was hungry. The generous visitor who had in previous years exhausted her substance upon this family was told that it was not necessary to visit them again just then, because we hoped to get them off shortly, and we would gladly call upon her for assistance, if any were required, but it seemed better that none should be given just then.

The result was unexpectedly successful. The kind friend who had taken the girl in hand was surprised at finding her at last amenable to her advice; and, in a week or two, the family was once more on the road,— this time outside the State lines,— and we hear that they are doing well. They pleaded for clothes and comforts for this their second journey; but we were afraid to trust them, and they went in their old clothes. The result is better than we feared. Every day they seem to be improving. The clergyman of the town, who was written to by the girl's friend, goes to see them, and is satisfied with their condition.

These stories, drawn from late experience,

illustrate what I have hinted at before,— that volunteer service is what we live by. We cannot, of course, get on in this work of investigation without some person whose business it is to be found regularly at certain hours, and upon whom we may all depend, because volunteer service must be interrupted service; but oftentimes, in making inquiries, the appeals of some one who is not known to have any business connection with any organization are of very great value, and will have far more influence than agents' letters.

How shall we increase this valuable volunteer service? "We are all members of one body working together," and a devoted agent said only a short time ago: "Pray make the visitors understand that, do the best I can, I may easily be mistaken; and I feel myself very dependent upon their impressions."

VII.

INTEMPERANCE.

"Tender pity for the poor has been a growing characteristic of this age. A better sign of it still is the increased sense of duty to them, not only as poor men, but as men. There needs, however, it appears to me, something still, before our charity shall be effectual for good. The feeling is there, the conscience is there; but there is wanting the wise thought and the resolute because educated will."

We have seen a degraded population increase year by year in our American cities. We have seen drunkenness decrease among our well-to-do people, and fall into a contempt unknown in the past century; but among the unprotected classes it has greatly increased, together with illiteracy and other evils, and yet we have continued to give broken food and "charity sewing" to our poor, and have felt that we have done what we could. In short, we have received the children of pauperized Europe into our open arms, and have wondered at first, then felt ourselves repelled, by the sad issue of our careless hospitality. Drunkenness is the root of a very large proportion of the suffering of the poor in the cities of America. Therefore, this is the chief problem with which the volunteer visitor as well as the political economist must deal. It is of no use to say, "I will have nothing to do with 'drunken cases,'" because here lies the ground of misery and of our labor. If "drunken cases" are to be excepted in any district, there can be no work of any moment done for the poor of that locality.

On the contrary, the visitor's motto should be, "Never give a family up." If the father drinks irrevocably, and will not support his family, he should be sentenced upon the visitor's testimony, and sent to some institution where he will be obliged to work. His wife may then be better able to do something for the support of the family. If the children are grown, they can assist her. If they are very young, they can be put into day-nurseries and kindergartens while she is at work, and return to her at night.

If the mother drinks, and cannot be influenced to reform, it will be far better for the children that she should be sent to the Reformatory at Sherburne (if she live in Boston), the visitor being willing to bear witness to what is known to be for the ultimate good of the family. If the father is dead or incapable of caring for his children, they may then be taken into "guardianship and custody" of the visitor or some other friend, and afterward placed out. Nevertheless, visitors continue to ask in these puzzling cases: "What can we do? Suppose the mother is respectable and intelligent, far above the average: can we let her and the six children suffer?"

Certainly, these sorrowful cases make us pause. There is great danger in yielding. If we clothe the children and give them food one day, the father will feel the situation less than before; and, unless we think best to support the family entirely, they will only sink lower as soon as our attention is engaged elsewhere. Something can be done, however; and much depends upon the visitor. The statutes of Massachusetts make it incumbent that a man should support his family. Therefore, we may call the arm of the law to assist us. A complaint to the police will sometimes do good, even if we go no farther; and, if we combine with such measures all the healthy and kindly influences we know, the whole current of affairs in that household may be gradually changed for the better.

We cannot afford either to fear or despise any labor in behalf of temperance. The evil runs too deep.

It is one of the visitor's duties to strive to enforce the laws of Massachusetts upon this question. The judge of the district may be asked to listen to the case and advise; the police of the district will assist, if requested, by keeping watch and threatening arrest; the truant officers will look in and see that the children are kept at school; and the visitor may meanwhile, by friendly oversight, interest the man in some club or friendly evening resort, where he will be withdrawn more or less from temptation. If he is too far gone and a slave to drink and, humanly speaking, incapable of reform, he must then be committed on long sentence to some institution. Such cases cannot be settled in a day nor in a year; but they are, perhaps, the most important branch of our labor: certainly, they are the most puzzling and difficult part of it.

"How many women," I asked a friend who conducted me lately over the Reformatory for women at Sherburne, "were sent here for drunkenness?" "Directly or indirectly, it has been the cause of nearly all the commitments," was the reply. "There are very few exceptions." It has been estimated that nine-tenths of the city poor who ask public relief have fallen into pauperism from the same cause. Let us accept our burden of work, therefore, with our eyes open and with hands willing to struggle with this evil.

It is not encouraging work in the present condition of our license law; but, even when all is done that law can do, there will still be no restraining force to compare with that of public opinion and a recognition of the divine law planted in the heart of men. Much remains to be done by visitors among the poor (who are beginning to create public opinion), by the knowledge they obtain daily. Mr. James H. Dormer, of Buffalo, writes: "Bishop Ireland, one of the most earnest, practical, and beautiful characters that ever formally identified himself with the temperance cause, has said:—

> What is at once practicable and would be most serviceable in diminishing the evils of intemperance is to demand of liquor-sellers high license fees. There are two grounds upon which we base our plea for high license. One is the economic ground. If a traffic of

any kind puts unusual impediments in the wheels of government, State or municipal, and increases to an inordinate degree its expenses, the traffic should be made to bear its due proportion of those expenses. Before saloon-keepers have reason to complain of injustice or harsh treatment, they should be made to pay over three-fourths of all sums spent annually in maintaining police forces, criminal courts, jails, and public charities. In allowing them to pay but trifles of those sums, the State or city is guilty of deep injustice toward the sober citizen, who is taxed to repair the harm inflicted by liquor upon society. The second ground for high license is the moral consideration that it is the duty of the government to prevent as well as to punish wrong-doing, when no principle is violated by such prevention, and to put restrictions upon a traffic which is dangerous to public morals. Saloons are numerous beyond all justification, and in most cases are in the hands of reckless individuals. High license will reduce the number. Not many who would be candidates for a bar could pay $1,000 or $500; nor would the wholesale dealer be anxious, as he is now, to advance the license fee. High license would drive saloons from the outlying districts into the more central portions of the city, where police control is more effective. It would end the unholy alliance between groceries and liquor, and the poor laborer or his wife could buy a pound of tea or sugar without being invited to buy also a glass of whiskey or beer. The impecunious fellows, ashamed to beg and too idle to work, willing, however, to sell whiskey, are often the men most careless of consequences: their idea is to make money. They would be kept out of the business. A salutary fear would rest upon all liquor-dealers of violating city ordinances, lest they lose their license, which has some value when it costs $500 or $1,000. Nor would so many drink, if we had high license. There are men who will seek out whiskey or beer wherever it is, and pay any money for it. There are many others, however, who will not drink, when temptation is not thrust upon them. The poor workingman, after his day's work, will not walk several blocks to find a saloon. If it is next door, and the selfish keeper, envying the dollar he has earned so hard, invites him with a sickly smile and a shake of his clammy hand to cross its threshold, the poor man will yield and get drunk. Diminish the saloons, and you diminish the number of drinkers. A low license fee is an open encouragement to the indefinite and irresponsible multiplication of rum-holes in every street and in every block of our cities.

Canon Farrar, in speaking of the effect of drunkenness upon the lives of children, enumerates nine results, one only more terrible than the last. The passage reads briefly as follows: —

"1st. They are exposed to shameful neglect. . . .

"2d. To horrible accidents. . . .

"3d. To cruelty. . . . A week ago, a drunken woman is seen holding a child of five months by the legs. When remonstrated with, she flings the child on the pavement, and runs away.

"4th. Not only to cruelty, but to death. A

fortnight ago, a child is found burned and scalded to death, because the drunken woman in charge of it falls against a fireplace....

"5th. They are exposed to dreadful *congenital sickness.* The author of *John Halifax* writes, after a visit to the East London Hospital for Children: 'The nurse said, "These are our worst and most painful cases." One felt in going through this ward that death was better than life.'

"6th. They are exposed also to murder....

"7th. And to *unconscious suicide.* In the joy of men this last Christmas, a child of three gets out of bed, drinks some whiskey left on the table, and in the morning is found dead.

"8th. They are exposed to something still worse,— that is, *sin....* How often are the children of the drunkard trained in sin!...

"9th. Lastly, how fearful is the lot of the drunkard's children from the fearful taint in the blood, the awful *hereditary craving!*"...

"With regard to the connection between intemperance and lunacy," writes Mr. Francis Peek, "the most eminent doctors connected with lunatic asylums put down at least twenty per cent. of the cases treated by them to intemperance."...

Mr. Peek continues: "If there be one duty

which is universally acknowledged as more incumbent than another on the governing power in a State, it is the duty of providing protection for the citizens. . . . In what way, then, can State action be taken with the best chance of success? . . . It is fairly proved that undue facilities for obtaining strong drink, involving those numberless inducements which competition compels dealers to offer in the shape of amusements, etc., are the greatest cause of national intemperance; that, where there are no drinking places, there is scarcely any intemperance at all; that, where there are few, there is very little; and that, where these facilities have been reduced, a corresponding decrease in intemperance has taken place. It is in evidence that where a public house has been introduced into a hitherto sober community, where none had before existed, drunkenness has followed. It is to the diminution of drinking facilities, and the discouragement of liquors of high alcoholic strength, that we must chiefly look for any improvement in this matter. . . .

"Every inducement is required for redoubled efforts to enlighten public opinion. . . . Every Band of Hope formed is a gain. . . . The battle must be won by degrees, by steady persistence and patient endeavor, by bringing public opinion to approve each step attained." ...

I promised in the earlier pages of this little book to refer again to the effect produced by Mrs. X.'s gift to a well-known relief society. Application had been made at the office of that society by Mary Conolly, a good-looking Irishwoman, for shoes and coal. She had three little children, and her husband had been out of work several weeks. The busy visitor, who not infrequently makes twenty visits a day, looked in upon the family at ten o'clock in the morning. He found the mother sleepy and uncombed, the room cold, the three children guiltless of face-washing, the room rather cleaner than the worst, however, but the man still asleep in bed in an adjoining room. "Poor man!" Mary said. "He was looking for work all day, it being very scarce now; and he had taken cold, which made his legs stiff." The eldest boy had just come in with a basket of cinders and some chips to make a fire. They were in debt for rent, they all needed shoes, and "Whatever we shall do if Mike don't find work soon I don't know. I ain't used to livin' so." And indeed it seemed as if she were not. So the visitor withdrew, marked it a worthy case, sent five dollars' worth of coal and shoes, and heard nothing more of the family until the next season, when the woman returned, representing still greater need, because there was another baby and work had been more scarce than ever.

It is hardly reasonable to expect a woman with three young children and a healthy husband to go to work, in order to get money for their support. Indeed, it is far from desirable. The best the visitor can do is to leave word for the man to come to see him, making an early appointment. Even in the hardest seasons, it is possible to get more or less work for men who are willing. Meanwhile, hard as it may seem, "relief" must absolutely be withheld as a general rule. If the man finds that the truant officer will get shoes for his children and societies will send him coal and he can get broken food at ten cents a day from hotels, which is sufficient to nourish his family, he will not make the same exertion to get and keep employment, and saving will be altogether out of his calculation; but, if his children are kept in the public schools less well clothed than other children, if he finds the room cold and the table bare when he goes home, his pride and comfort will both be at stake, and, if the man be not sunk too low, these motives will be found strong levers for his regeneration.

Either something can be done to bring a man to his senses and give him a chance once more to face the world as an honest man should, or, if all available means fail to restore him, he must be put away where he will no longer continue to contaminate society. Something is to be done in either case.

The man can be put to work, and by kindness, personal influence, opportunity, reform clubs, combined with watchfulness of the police and truant officers, can be kept in order, or he cannot; and, in the latter case, he should not be suffered to lie in his bed by day and contaminate the community by night, but he should be brought under the penalty of the laws of the Commonwealth. This last work is usually considered as outside of the pale of charity work, but it is as much a part of it and as great a necessity as any other part. It cannot be left to the police altogether to do this. The visitor is often needed to make the complaint or to appear as witness. Who should know better than such a friend the suffering caused to a little family by the father's sins and self-indulgence? Who can be so well qualified to speak in their behalf? I have in mind such a family at this moment, where the priest performed this benevolent office with the assistance of the truant officer. The father and mother both drank, and the children were neglected. Both parents were shut up in separate institutions and the children taken away from them; but, after two months, they were suffered to have home and children again. The result has been satisfactory. The man is at work all day, the woman at home, their debts are paid, their rooms are decent; and the wholesome fear which hangs over them in case of failure, combined with the unceasing kindness and attention of the priest, have thus far kept them from falling.

It would be far from impossible to give many touching and interesting stories in this place of what has been effected by the personal influence of good men and women over those who are weak and subject to temptation; but the private nature of such work, as well as lack of space, must prevent. I know a certain Captain of our Police who has saved at least one man, not by the force of the law, but by exercising his private influence alone. The man in question had brought his family to starvation, and he was in a condition to be arrested; but he is now a respected and self-respecting carpenter, his family restored to their comfortable home.

A lady who had striven patiently, but, as it seemed, unsuccessfully, with many cases of intemperance, lost no courage, but helped a man who still continued to drink at intervals, until she feared she might be doing harm rather than good by her renewed forgiveness of his broken promises. The period arrived when she saw that further help should be withdrawn; and before a solemn company gathered "in an upper chamber" prayers were offered for his future, and he was told that, in justice to others, nothing further could be done for him. He was a man above the lower classes of the poor; but he had sold his clothes, and had crept in to the back of the room in the wretched overalls provided in lieu of clothes by the refuge where he had found shelter. When all was silent, he asked to be heard; and, kneeling there, he thanked God for these friends who had been so patient with him. His own family had long felt they could have no influence over him. Then, he besought our Father in heaven to give him strength to resist temptation. He had tried again and again. Would not the Infinite God help to save him, when all earthly hope seemed withdrawn? Perfect silence and the raining down of tears followed his sorrowful figure as he withdrew, and the patient woman who continued to be his friend determined still to endeavor to sustain him in his new resolve. He was no longer young, the habit was an old one; but from that moment, which is now three years ago, he has been perfectly sober, is restored to his position and his family, and this dark valley is to the world as if it had never been.

VIII.

VISITORS AND VISITED.

"You probably all know," writes Miss Octavia Hill, "that dirt disappears gradually in places that cleanly people go in and out of frequently."

One of the first duties of a visitor is to use the senses in entering a tenement house. The laws of the city of Boston are very clear about the care which must be taken in order to preserve the public health and public decency, and the officers of the Board of Health are courteous and attentive in listening to and following up suggestions. We wish all persons assuming the responsibility of visitors would recognize that it is a part of their duty to give a report concerning the condition of the houses they enter. The following extracts from the Statutes show how great a reform we can bring about by faithful reporting, accompanied by a personal request that the law shall be enforced: —

8. The board or the health officer shall order the owner or occupant at his own expense to remove any

nuisance, source of filth, or cause of sickness, found on private property, within twenty-four hours....

10. If the owner or occupant fails to comply with such order, the board may cause the nuisance, source of filth, or cause of sickness to be removed; and all expenses incurred thereby shall be paid by the owner, occupant, or other person who caused or permitted the same, if he has had actual notice from the board of health of the existence thereof....

109. Every tenement or lodging house shall have in every room which is occupied as a sleeping-room, and which does not communicate directly with the external air, a ventilating or transom window. Every such house or building shall have in the roof, at the top of the hall, an adequate and proper ventilator, of a form approved by the inspector of buildings.

110. Every such house shall be provided with a proper fire-escape, or means of escape in case of fire, to be approved by the inspector of buildings.

111. The roof of every such house shall be kept in good repair and so as not to leak; and all rain-water shall be so drained or conveyed therefrom as to prevent its dripping on ground or causing dampness in the walls, yard, or area. *All stairs shall be provided with proper balusters or railings, and shall be kept in good repair.*

112. Every such building shall be provided with good and sufficient water-closets, earth-closets, or privies, of a construction approved by the inspector of buildings, and shall have proper doors, traps, soil-pans, and other suitable works and arrangements, so far as may be necessary, to insure the efficient operation thereof. It shall not be lawful, without a permit from the board of health or superintendent of health, to let or

occupy, or suffer to be occupied separately as a dwelling, any vaults, cellar, or underground room.... The owner or keeper of any lodging-house, and the owner or lessee of any tenement house or part thereof, shall *whitewash the walls and ceilings thereof twice at least every year*, in the months of April and October, unless the said board shall otherwise direct. Every *tenement or lodging-house shall have legibly posted or painted on the wall or door in the entry, or some public accessible place, the name and address of the owner or owners and of the agent or agents, or* any one having charge of the renting and collecting of the rents for the same....

These extracts from the laws may be found in a little pamphlet printed by the Board of Health and perfectly accessible. From these brief quotations, it will be seen how large a power the visitor possesses. Contrast for a moment what may be done with what is done, and no one can fail to see great possibilities of improvement. If walls and ceilings must be whitewashed twice in the year, why do we find them so black? If balusters and railings must be kept in repair, why do we climb up uneven stairs by a broken rail? If there must always be a ventilating or transom window leading to the outer air, why do we stifle among smells too bad to remember? The answer is easy. There has been no one to complain. Landlords are apt to let things alone as long as they can, and these evils have grown to be what they are by the visitor's default.

We pray the friends of the poor to remember this. Helen Campbell says: "In one tenement house in New York, seven hundred and fifty people were so packed that each family had a living space of but ten feet by eleven. The Chinese quarter of San Francisco shows nothing worse. . . . In 1870, an Act of Parliament demolished ten thousand houses in Glasgow, and within two years a marked change in health returns, prevention of crime, and arrest and conviction of offenders was the result. . . . It is in the tenement houses that we must seek for the mass of the poor. And it is in the tenement houses that we find the causes which, combined, are making of the generation now coming up a terror in the present and a promise of future evil beyond man's power to reckon. They are a class apart, retaining all the most brutal characteristics of the Irish peasant at home, but without the redeeming light-heartedness, the tender impulses, and strong affections of that most perplexing people. . . .

"There are many houses with every plank in them steeped in sin and misery. Law should be strong enough to order their destruction. ... We think the time of coarse, brutal sinning is over, and that our charities, our great hospitals, our missions here and there, set us apart from and beyond any century that has gone before. We wonder why pauperism has become a profession; and we build stately asylums for our idiots and insane and crippled, while we allow thousands of hot-beds for the production of such species to do their work under our very eyes. If it goes on at the present rate, ten asylums must rise where one stands now, and State taxes double and treble to cover the cost per head of what one might judge to be a personal luxury, each tax-payer requiring his special pauper or idiot, as kings once had their own particular fool.

"Foul air and overcrowding would, however, be less fatal in its results, were food understood. The well-filled stomach gives strange powers of resistance to the body. ... Happily, to know an evil is to have taken the first step in its eradication. ... To have made cooking and industrial training the fashion, is to have cleared away the thorny underbrush on that debatable ground, the best education of the poor. ... That cooking schools and the knowledge of cheap and savory preparation of food must soon have their effect on the percentage of drunkards no one can question. Philanthropists may urge what reforms they will,— less crowding, purer air, better sanitary regulations,— but this question of food underlies all. The knowledge that is broad enough to insure good food is broad enough to mean better living in all ways. . . . Such work must be done from within, out. Methods which touch merely the outside are but of temporary service. One woman who has learned in any degree to order her own home and life aright will be more a power with those among whom that life passes than a dozen average preachers; and, if the rich would trust less to indiscriminate giving and more to the work of some accredited agent of this description, they would find double the result for every investment.

"How to make even the smallest home clean and attractive, and to get the largest return from every dollar earned, is a knowledge that means physical salvation, and thus a better prospect for understanding the spiritual. . . . The training school is even more important than the public school, and *industrial education* the only solution of the incompetence and well-nigh hopeless inefficiency of the poorer classes.

"They are with us. The burden is ours, and cannot be cast aside. It remains with us to train them into decent members of society, or to fold our hands and let the crowd of imbeciles and drunkards and criminals and lunatics increase year by year, till suddenly some frightful social convulsion opens the eyes that have refused to see, and disaster brings about what moderate effort could long before have accomplished."

There are hundreds of tenement houses in every poor ward of Boston, where the evils of pauperized Europe seem to be fostered by transplanting. Something more can be done by a better fulfilling of the laws and closer official oversight. Nothing, however, can compare with the influence of a friend who is also landlord or landlady, enforcing extreme punctuality in the payment of rents and proper care of the apartments rented. "When a tenant is out of work, instead of reducing his energy by any gifts of money, we simply, whenever the funds at our disposal allow it, employ him in restoring and purifying the houses. . . . The same cheering and encouraging sort of influence, though in a less degree, is exercised by our plan of having a little band of scrubbers. We have each passage scrubbed twice a week by one of the elder girls. The sixpence thus earned is a stimulus, and they often take an extreme interest in the work itself. . . .

"Among the many benefits which the possession of the houses enables us to confer on the people, perhaps the most important is our power of saving them from neighbors who would render their lives miserable. It is a most merciful thing to protect the poor from the pain of living in the next room to drunken, disorderly people. 'I am dying,' said an old woman to me the other day. 'I wish you would put me where I can't hear S. beating his wife.'. . . Occasionally, we come upon people whose lives are so good and sincere it is only by such services and the sense of our friendship that we can help them at all. In all important things, they do not need our teaching, while we may learn much from them."

For the assistance of the visitor who can give only a small portion of time to the work, a sheet has been printed asking to have certain simple questions answered relating to the condition of the house or houses where the people live who are visited. The little paper may be found at the office of the Associated Charities in Boston.

In considering the need of destroying certain dwellings altogether, we find that Mr. Charles Spencer, of Philadelphia, has lately said: —

If the question be asked, What has become of the wretched people, have they been driven into other districts, or has their manner of life been improved correspondingly with the better accommodations supplied? we answer that we have not learned that the bettering of Bedford Street has made any other district worse; but, on the contrary, since the people have been scattered, we have known in some happy instances of those who have been forced to leave, driven out from dens of vice, and having settled in less noxious localities, becoming industrious and respectable citizens.

Mr. Theodore Starr thus speaks of what he believes to be a reasonably successful endeavor to come into contact with the laboring poor as their landlord, and by fair treatment, by a consideration of their needs, and by insisting upon a faithful performance of their obligations, to gain an influence over them which, it was hoped, might lead to much physical, moral, and spiritual improvement of their condition. The basis of the experiment was a purely business one, and its object was twofold: —

1. Could houses of a reasonable size, rented at such a rate as to induce the laboring man

to use them, be made to return a fair interest to the owner?

2. Could the slums of the city be redeemed to decent living, if decent houses were built and owned by decent people, and rented to decent laboring men?

"I should like to emphasize," he writes, "the character of the opposition to the work of regeneration. It arises from three sources,— the old style of property owners, the rum-seller, and the ward politician. So long as the work is that of simply visiting the poor and relieving such cases as seem to need help, the visitor is unmolested and arouses no opposition; but let one blow, *however feeble, be struck at the root of the matter, and at once a coalition is formed to obstruct the work.* . . . He who enlists in this war for the regeneration of the slums must do so in the face of bitter opposition, deep discouragement, and oft-repeated disappointment, for indeed he 'wrestles against principalities, against powers, against the rulers of the darkness of this world, against spiritual wickedness in high places.' Nevertheless, if he will but persevere in the right methods to the end, his effort cannot fail to be crowned with an enduring success."

One of the earliest and most important topics which should engage the attention of the visitor is that of helping people to save. In Newport, this branch of work has been made a specialty, the peculiar circumstances of so large a watering-place rendering it a question of prime importance. The committee began in the spring of 1880 to warn their poor friends that they would not be allowed to receive public relief the following winter, and that, unless they meant to suffer, they must lay up something in summer for the winter's wants. The plan adopted is simple in its details, and is given in full in their report for the benefit of those who wish to follow it. It is unusual, even in these days of good work, to see any plan followed quite so closely and carefully by a company of visitors; and the result is a success beyond all anticipation. Surely, if our workers everywhere would read this report, the methods would be much more widely adopted. In conclusion, the secretary writes:—

We are ready to say, however, that having educated our people (or some of them) into the practice of saving, our wish is to see them strong enough to turn the practice into a habit, and to do without our help. For this reason, we look with great satisfaction on the prospect of post-office savings banks, which will make the matter easy for them; and more than a year ago we signed a petition to the Postmaster-General for the establishment of such banks.

"Saving is like spending," writes Mrs. Ames, "more and more easy the longer it is practised. It is also a conservative moral habit which helps to set in order the whole life. It is a great gain when these people are once aroused to the fact that they can save."

Trouble of any kind, and especially any misfortune which has a tendency to lower a person in the social scale, drives people into solitude. Edward Denison wrote, "How many thousands of paupers have lived and died and been buried at the public expense, whom a little friendly advice, a little search for friends or relatives, some pains taken to find proper work, when the first application to the Board was made, would have lifted out of the mire and set on the rock of honest industry." Many of the poor who most deeply need visitors are lonely persons, and the fact of finding a friend at last is encouragement to them and a beginning of better times. The influence of clubs, unions, associations, meetings for discussion, is often very beneficial. Men whose homes are uncomfortable are helped over many a hard hour by being allowed to go to a reading-room or good place of resort. There are so many bad places to go to that the sooner the visitor can put a half-discouraged man into relation to an organization worth joining the better chance there will be of his improvement.

In an admirable little English book, by Ellice Hopkins, called *Work among Workingmen*, we read: "One thing at least is certain. The public house, in some form or other, is a necessity.... However domestic a man may be, he requires the society of his fellows, he needs some place where he can see the papers, and where he can talk trade and politics.... The club house is an absolute necessity to workingmen.... Practically, it seems to be constantly overlooked that the old tavern bore precisely the same fruits in the well-to-do class as it is now bearing in the lower classes; and not till the club took the place of the tavern did a better state of public opinion arise, and a consequent diminution of drunkenness.... Should we not meet with more success, if we were steadily to recognize that the club, with its absence of vicious self-interest enlisted in the drink traffic, with its *esprit de corps* and its character to sustain, does present, both positively and negatively, the necessary moral influences to control the use of intoxicants, or to dispense with them altogether, as may be thought best; and if, while still endeavoring to procure an amendment of our licensing laws, we were to throw our chief energies into getting the club substituted for the public house?

"'Why not advocate the establishment of coffee-palaces which are open to all?' some one will ask. 'Why restrict it to the members of a club?'

"Coffee-palaces are admirable things, and I advocate their being multiplied tenfold in every large town. They will do much to educate everybody out of our present ridiculous dependence on alcoholic drinks, as if they were the necessary concomitant of every social and kindly feeling.... As a rule, however, workingmen do not use them as an evening resort, for the simple reason that they do not afford quiet, separate rooms where they can feel at home, and where they can smoke their pipes and do as they like. And I would earnestly point out, it is the evening resort that must ever be the stronghold of drunkenness.... Even in those rare cases where the upper premises of a coffee-palace are let off for the exclusive use of a workingmen's club, there is the great disadvantage of the club being forced to adopt total abstinence principles, whether they wish it or not, since intoxicants are not allowed on the premises. In the case of voluntary teetotalers, this would lead to no evil; but, with those who are not, it leads to their going elsewhere to get the glass of beer they cannot procure at their club. And I would again urge that you should never attack drunkenness in the mass on principles of total abstinence. ... Why do we expect of workingmen a self-denial which, in the mass, we do not practise ourselves? ... When you admit intoxicants, you must also secure a moral element, the social *esprit de corps* of a well-organized club, to control them. The admission of beer into coffee-palaces would, I fear, generate the old abuses over again."

"The workingman's home," writes Edward Denison again, "in great towns is such that he cannot there give himself either to study or recreation. He must have a club; and, till every head of a family belongs to a club, there is not much hope of the poorer artisans improving their condition." Women and children, too, should be introduced into the schools and classes working everywhere for their education, physical, moral, and religious.

They need to be persuaded to take the first step; but, this difficult point once passed, they are willing to make a good deal of effort to hold the places they have gained.

The old method of working for the poor always left the man in the swamp, but threw him biscuits to keep him from starving. By means of throwing him biscuits enough, he managed to make the oozy place appear to himself soft and even comfortable. The new method is to throw him a plank. He cannot eat or drink the plank, but he can scramble out upon it, and have his share of the labors and rewards which the experience of life brings both to high and low.

"The supreme need is to give not only our dollars, but ourselves, and to learn the business."

The noble duty of caring for the sick poor is one which has been omitted from these pages, because of the importance of the subject and the fact that it is too often considered altogether as a specialty; but there are certain things which every woman should know, and which, if she visits without knowing, she cannot fulfil all her duty. Miss Nightingale writes as follows regarding the success to be attained by nurses who serve the sick poor:—

As to your success? What is not your success? To raise the homes of your patients, so that they never fall back again to dirt and disorder,— such is your nurses' influence. To pull through life and death cases,— cases which it would be an honor to pull through with all the appurtenances of hospitals, or of the richest of the land,— and this without any appurtenances at all. To keep whole families out of pauperism by preventing the home from being broken up, and by nursing the bread-winner back to health. To drag the noble art of nursing out of the sink of relief doles. To carry out practically the principles of preventing disease by stopping its causes or infections which spread disease.

Florence Craven says upon this subject:—

Whenever a nurse enters, order and cleanliness must enter with her. She must reform and re-create, as it were, the homes of the sick poor. These unfortunate people often lose even the feeling of what it is to be clean. The district nurse has, therefore, to show them their room clean for once, and to bring about this result with her own hands; to sweep and dust, empty and wash out all the appalling dirt and foulness; air and disinfect, rub the windows, sweep the fireplace, carry out and shake the bits of old sacking and carpet and lay them down again, fetch fresh water, and fill the kettle, wash the patient and the children, and make the bed.

And Miss Nightingale adds again:—

Every room thus cleaned has always been kept so. This is her glory. She found it a pigsty: she left it a tidy, airy room.

To teach the poor how to use even the small share of goods and talents intrusted to them proves to be almost the only true help of a worldly sort which it is possible to give them. Other gifts, through the long ages tried and found wanting, we must have done with. Nearly one million of dollars in public and private charities have been given away in one year in Boston alone; and this large sum has brought, by way of return, a more fixed body of persons who live upon the expectation of public assistance, and whose degradation becomes daily deeper. The truth has been made clear to us that expenditure of money and goods alone does not alleviate poverty.

How, then, we ask, may help be given? To find a fitting answer, we have studied the methods of other countries and of holy, self-sacrificing men and women who have also learned wisdom in their humble devotion to their work. And the answer we find is this: we have followed the law, and not the spirit of the Master; but the law is dead, and he still lives among us, the shepherd of his sheep, speaking through these hungry and suffering children, and praying us not to give the meat which perisheth, but the meat which shall endure. In our comfortable and sheltered homes, we forget how near these wretched cellars and attics are to the reformatories and prison cells. They are the next door, and it depends often upon our personal influence over the poor to keep that door shut.

When we are told that certain evils cannot be helped, that we may as well let things alone, we must remember that experience has taught differently. Evils can be helped, and to let things alone is to lend ourselves to wrong. It is to be cowardly and to hate just where we are taught to love, and to have faith that will remove mountains.

It is impossible to overestimate the value of friendly communication with the poor and unfortunate. When I see what is accomplished sometimes by what in contrast may be called so small an expenditure, it seems impossible not to spread the good news, and thus bring in a very much larger number of workers, where the harvest is so abundant. "From wealth, little can be hoped; from intercourse, everything."

www.ingramcontent.com/pod-product-compliance
Lightning Source LLC
Chambersburg PA
CBHW020116170426
43199CB00009B/549